Pursue, Overtake and Recover All

By

Bishop R.D. Brown, DD.

Copyright © 2023 Bishop R.D. Brown, DD.

All rights reserved. This book or any portion thereof may not be reproduced or used in any manner whatsoever without the express written permission of the publisher except for the use of brief quotations in a book review.

ABOUT THE AUTHOR

I am currently President/CEO of **World of Power Ministries Inc.**, an international non-profit organization with both national and international functions. In that capacity, I have been fortunate enough to travel the world spreading the gospel and ministering to those in need. From the United States to Canada, South America, Europe, Asia, Africa, and the Caribbean Islands, I have tirelessly promoted the gospel of hope.

My passion for making a difference goes beyond my work in ministry. With a Bachelor's Degree in Biblical Studies, a Master's Degree in Ministry and a Doctor's Degree in Divinity, I have dedicated my life to learning and sharing that knowledge with others. I am also a Board-Certified Counselor, operating in that capacity as a licensed counselor for psychological health, family counseling and substance abuse.

I have established facilities to care for wayward teens, the elderly, and children, including Boys Home facilities, Senior Citizens facilities and Grace Academy, a licensed Day Care Center. I have worked with organizations like Habitat for Humanity and Coats for Kids to provide housing and winter clothing for those in need. And during the pandemic, I partnered with local food ministries to feed tens of thousands of families.

DEDICATION

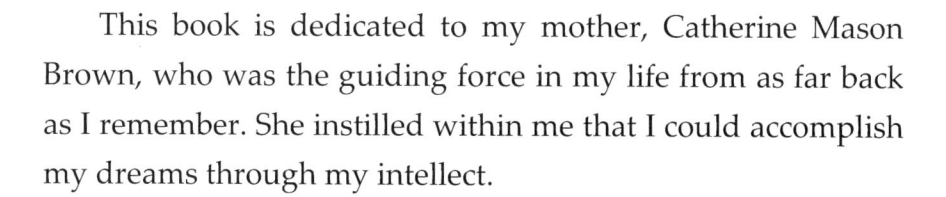

This book is dedicated to my mother, Catherine Mason Brown, who was the guiding force in my life from as far back as I remember. She instilled within me that I could accomplish my dreams through my intellect.

When my professional football career was sidelined because of an inoperable injury, she said these words to me when I felt hopeless concerning my future. "You still have a mind." Those words have guided me to this point in my life and to the authorship of this book.

ACKNOWLEDGMENTS

I want to acknowledge with a sincere debt of gratitude, Barbara Koggu, for consistently pushing me to author this book. She has been relentless in encouraging me toward this end. Thank you from the depths of my heart.

To my sister, Myrtle Brown Ross, who has been supportive in helping me to fund this project and for the wisdom she shared with me towards marketing concepts.

To my daughter, Alana N. Brown, who helped in determining the final book cover and critiquing other areas of the design.

To the World of Power Ministries Inc. staff and congregants; There are too many to mention by name but here are just a few chartered members: T'Shanna Long-Young, Facilitator, Roy Young, Deacon, Anele Young, Posthumously, Mother Carrie Long, Dr. Curtis Wigging, Pastor; and all the Hot Springs, Arkansas Ministry; Wanda Bodden, Pastor and Sports Director - Bringing Back The Glory, Port Arthur, Texas and all the Church of the Overflow Ministry, Elder Tonja Sesley, Memphis Urban League President and CEO, and The Memphis, Tennessee Ministry; Gwendolyn Edwards, Minister Sheridan Smotherman, Minister Brenda Payne, The Longview area, Minister Delphine Andrews, Prayer Minister, The Tyler

Ministry...Elder Barbara Koggu and Reginald Koggu, Ifeyni Koggu, Christy Shackleford, President/CEO Christy's Safe Haven, Kendrick Shackleford, Jordan Shackleford, Mary Starling, Photographer/Alms Chairperson, Shella Coleman, Praise Minister, Hospitality Team: Gillian Brown, Peggy Tave, Shavonda Collins, Food Distributer, Dorinda Williams, Tangela Kennedy, Mary Ransom, The Dallas/Fort Worth/Arlington Area, Fannie Kate Williams, The Church Mother of World of Power Ministries, Deborah Huckabee and Vion Huckabee, Vikki White, Hospitality, Tai Grey, Robert White, Cassandra Landrum, Social Media Director, The Gilmer Group, Deacon Ronald Slaughter, Pam Slaughter. The Big Sandy Ministry, Pastor Alfred White and Shepherdess Tammie White.

And finally, to Jane, my publishing agent and her entire team. Thanks.

Table of Contents

ABOUT THE AUTHOR iii
DEDICATION v
ACKNOWLEDGMENTS vi
INTRODUCTION x
    The Inevitability of Loss 1
    Recovery of the Promise 2
    Understanding Foreordained Promises 3
    The Bible Deed 10
    Recovery Through the Word of Promise 21
    Get It Back 22
    Jesus Teaches in Parables 23
    The Deliverance of Restoration 34
    A Time of Loss 54
    How Did I Get into This Mess, and How Do I Get Out? 59
    Zik lag – Zig-Zag 85
    The Circle of Life 87
    Seasons of Recovery 89
    The Third Day 89
    Gimel 92
    The Fire at Zik lag 94

The Season of Change 96
Obstacles to Recovery 98
Methodology of Recovery 99
Self-Courage 99
Overcoming Grief 100
Intercession 102
The Ephod 104
Prophetic Prayer 104
The Praises of Israel 105
God's Answer 109
Find your Egyptian! 111
Mentoring 112
Coincidence or Purpose 112
Gifts 113
The Six Hundred 113
The Four Hundred 115
The Battle for Recovery 115
The Strategy for Battle 116
Total Recovery For All 117
David's New Law 118
Overflow 119

INTRODUCTION

I am writing this book at a time when the United States and the world have experienced one of the greatest losses in modern history. We are in the year 2023 post-pandemic and many people are grappling with the aftereffects of massive loss. First and foremost is the loss of physical life. From January 3, 2020, to April 26, 2023, there have been 103,081,453 confirmed cases of COVID-19, with 1,121,819 deaths reported to (WHO) World Health Organization. Loss of this nature is a subject that must be approached with a delicate and compassionate perspective because of the emotional trauma that is attached to the loss of a loved one.

Although I am a Board-Certified Counselor trained in grief counseling, it is still difficult to bring comfort to those who have lost mothers and fathers, sisters and brothers, children and kindred, co-workers and friends in an untimely way. In that capacity, I have been privileged to counsel many and I say privileged because I personally know the pain of that particular loss when loved ones can no longer share phone conversations or holiday dinners and family gatherings. Yes, it is, in my estimation, one of the most severe pains of loss that must be dealt with in order to recover.

Still, it is a subject that I believe should be redressed within both the secular as well as the Christian community. Although I have the formal training to redress this loss, I must admit that I sometimes feel inadequate. Nevertheless, with the help of my God, I will endeavor to help the readers find comfort, guidance, and restoration in the effort to recover all. Additionally, l have counseled others regarding loss materially, socially, psychologically, and spiritually.

Needless to say, this book is for anyone who has suffered a loss.

The estimated cumulative financial costs of the COVID-19 pandemic related to the lost output health reduction total costs is estimated at more than $16 Trillion or roughly 90% of the annual GDP of the United States. For a family of four, the estimated loss would be nearly $200,000. The U.S. GDP fell by 8.9% in the second quarter of 2020; the largest single-quarter contraction in more than 70 years. In 2020, 6% of the nation's businesses failed, 9.7% postponed, and 8.2% decreased, and 1.5% increased some of their budgeted capital expenditures during the coronavirus pandemic. All of these statistics were at an alarming rate, and many have not recovered to date. You do not have to be an economist to understand the appalling loss our country suffered, and most other countries did not fare as well as the United States. Most of us are still feeling the aftereffects of the pandemic through shortages, rent and housing increases, automobile prices increase, gas and oil price increases, and grocery and appliance increases.

I have served in ministry in the Christian church in various capacities for fifty years and as a Diocesan Bishop over numerous churches both within the United States and abroad.

My findings are unadorned with perplexity and easy to communicate. Everyone that I have spoken with has experienced some form of loss. The untimely death of a loved one through sickness, accidents, or gun violence. One-time lovers found themselves no longer in love and in the middle of a horrific divorce with all the drama of a Hollywood feature presentation. Some lost cars to the repo man, banks, theft, or vehicular crashes. Others lost lifetime wealth in the stock market, 401k, or various investment opportunities. Homeowners lost their American dream to foreclosure, waking up one morning, packing up, and leaving the place that had served as more than just a residence but a home. Sudden physiological handicaps and unexpected health issues, both physical and emotional, have caused drastic and inconceivable changes in their lifestyles. Others had their freedoms taken away through incarceration, and whether justly or unjustly, their loss of freedom was horrific. It did not matter whether they were innocent or not. As a matter of fact, the loss was more devastating when the loss was suffered while they were innocent. Unwarranted police murders of its citizens have escalated and left many feeling hopeless about their loss. Furthermore, natural disasters, from floods, tornadoes, hurricanes, and earthquakes, have added new dimensions of psychological complexity as well as physical and material loss. The list would be prolonged if I continued to share the knowledgeable accounts that I have been privy to. If you happen to be in one or several of those categories, let us start the journey to recovery and restoration. ***Let us pursue, overtake and recover all!!!***

We will not sing a song of woe concerning loss but will nevertheless answer specific questions, come to a resolve and eventually discover methodologies of complete recovery and restoration. In this discourse, we will ask the questions "why" as well as "how" loss occurs and find the answers to complete recovery.

The Inevitability of Loss

Loss is a touchy subject, especially in Christendom, one that is ambivalent even to the most devout Christian. It is one of those subjects that we either conceal in ignominy or wear as an insignia of the testament that we are one of the true believers of the Lord suffering in the semblance of Job but not to be spoken of publicly in the presence of our brothers and sisters.

It is as if it has become a badge of shame to even mention the loss in a culture that esteems goodliness with gain. It is adopted that if you are not living in dream houses, driving expenses automobiles, wearing name-brand clothing, and traveling at leisure, you must not be living right. That is just not so.

If we look at Bible believers, their stories were not written on flowery beds of ease.

Men and women of faith suffered afflictions and reproaches. They were thrown into lion pits. They had cruel mocking and scourgings, and some were bound and thrown into prisons. They were stoned, sawn asunder, and slain with the sword. They wandered in deserts and in mountains, and in dens and caves of the earth. They were destitute, afflicted, and tormented. Nevertheless, all of them received a good report. They were blessed and delivered. In their weakness, they were made strong. They conquered kingdoms and found inheritances in the promises of God.

Loss comes to us all in some form or the other. It is inevitable! It will happen today, tomorrow or next week, or next year. It happens to the rich, the poor, the intellectual, and the unlearned. My writings are to prepare you for it and help you to get through it and come out on the other side of it in victory and complete wholeness.

Recovery of the Promise

This is a book about recovery, not in the sense as it is used in substance abuse recovery, but recovery as it relates to the *substance* of *foreordained personal promises*. Those are the promises that you know in your inner being relate to your destiny. They are promises that you dream of repeatedly until the focus of your conscience and subconscious mind is saturated during your every waking moment as well as the comatose moments of heart and soul. You know in your knower that these are not the promises of men but promises of God. You know thorough, thoughtful contemplation that these are promises that you long for and live for. Even when the possession of these promises eludes you through a series of unfortunate events, whether through external forces or mistakes of your own volition, still, the undaunted desire is established in your soul and spirit that these promises are certain to be realized, and you will not be satisfied until they are manifested.

Understanding Foreordained Promises

Some of these things may sound foreign to some so, allow me to explain. In the writing of Peter in his first epistle, he speaks of redemption for the people of God that was foreordained. Foreordained is from a Greek word which means to know beforehand, to foreknow, and to choose based on that foreknowledge. It denotes more than foresight but connotes purpose. With that definition and inflection of the text, we understand that the purpose of the redeemed was determined before eternity. Furthermore, this supports the idea of predestination, as explained in the writing of Paul.

"God hath not cast away his people which he foreknew...." Romans 11:1. Again, he writes, *"Blessed be the God and Father of our Lord Jesus Christ, who hath blessed us with all spiritual blessings in heavenly places in Christ: According as he hath chosen us in him before the foundation of the world, that we should be holy and without blame before him in love: Having predestinated us to the adoption of children by Jesus Christ to himself, according to the good pleasure of his will, To the praise of the glory of his grace, wherein he hath made us accepted in the beloved." Ephesians 1:3-6*

It may seem a little difficult to grasp, but God, in His predetermined counsel, ordained promises for us who are now born into his kingdom even while we were sinners. This does not remove the will of man from the equation. It is, however, intended to bring security because of aligning the will of man with the plan and promises of God.

Some of the other persuasion believes that man has no will of his own, but I do not ascribe to that position. *For whom he did foreknow, he also did predestinate to be conformed to the image of his Son, that we might be the firstborn among many brethren. Moreover whom he did predestinate, them he also called: and whom he called, them he justified, and whom he justified, them he also glorified. What shall we then say to these things? If God be for us who can be against us? Romans 8:29-31.*

Predestination does not exclude us from responsibility; in fact, this teaching instructs us that we are more accountable. If God has provided all things for us to the point where we have the promise that we have been predestined by God to conform to the image of Christ, we have no way to justify our lack of spiritual maturity because the Lord has given us all things that pertain to life and godliness through Christ.

Legal Deed of Promise

These promises can be explained in the Greek language better than in the English language as we look at the word substance. In Hebrews 11:1, we find the theological definition of faith:

"Now, faith is the substance of things hoped for, the evidence of things not seen." It is not my intention to dissect this verse or do an exegesis now. Perhaps later, but we will focus exclusively on the meaning of the word **substance**. The word in the Greek language is hupostasis. In the English language, one of its primary meanings is translated as *assurance*. Another

meaning that relates to assurance is a written description of a title deed. In order to provide assurance, a written description of the promises is spelled out in detail. For all practical purposes, the assurance based on the written description of a title deed is more practical, and we will use that definition.

Those who are familiar with property terms or legal real estate vocabulary, immediately understand the implication. For those who are not, let me explain. Title deeds are documents showing ownership, as well as rights and obligations to the described property. A deed is a signed and, in some jurisdictions, usually sealed legal instrument in writing that is used to grant a right. They require the author's signature and, in some cases, a form of notarization or attesting witnesses.

Deeds are also referred to as contracts because they require the mutual agreement of more than one person. Though similar to the old English word, covenant, a covenant can be unilateral, in the sense of "un" from the Latin meaning one. A covenant can be a promise on the part of one person to another person without any kind of demands, commitments, or obligations from that person whatsoever. This is a term that I call unconditional in reference to the other party. It is unconditional in the respect that no conditions are required of that person. It can be termed a gift.

However, a covenant can also become a conditional and binding agreement, as in Hebrew and many other eastern cultures. The important thing to note about a deed versus a simple unconditional covenant is that it is enforceable without *consideration* - that being the concept of legal value in connection with the contract with the other party. It allows for a third-party beneficiary to enforce an undertaking in the deed as well as other benefits that I will explain later. In the simplest term, a deed is any formal document that confirms or transfers interest or right of ownership to an asset from one person to another.

There are some deeds that I would like to cite for a specific reference. These deeds are termed *Specialties*. They are contracts under seal or bond. They are not necessarily known by this name in the United States, but the function is generally the same as most of the property deeds of the States. I have cited this name for application references when I talk about spiritual deeds of promise in the following paragraph.

It is good to observe that this type of deed ranks above simple contracts, or unconditional covenants in the administration of a decedent's estate for *paying off liabilities*. Additionally, the limitation of *specialties* is *twice* the limitation period of a simple contract.

Let us go further. If the deed is of a specialty's nature, then it is a contract or covenant under *seal* or bond of law. It has a witness or witnesses and has administrative powers to pay off all debts with *double* the limitation of a single contract.

Before I go any further in a legal sense, allow me to elaborate and relate the operation of deeds to the application and concept of ownership. Then, we will look at rights and obligations as they relate to the property **described in writing** in the deed document. *That which is described in the document is what you own.* It is described in detail, meticulous in every respect. I have cited an actual legal deed as an example to bring clarity. The names are changed, and certain other information is omitted, but the idea will be conveyed.

VOL 1234 PAGE 214

ASSUMPTION WARRANTY DEED

STATE OF MISSOURI   ) (

) (

KNOW ALL MEN BY THESE PRESENTS

COUNTY OF   ) (

    THAT BACK IN POWER MINISTRIES, of the County of Cass, State of Missouri, hereinafter called "GRANTORS", whether one of more, for and in consideration of the TEN MILLION AND NO/100THS (10,000,000.00) DOLLARS and other good and valuable consideration, being the exchange of certain real property, the undersigned paid by ROBERT D. SMITH and wife KARLA G. SMITH, hereinafter called "GRANTEES", whether one or more, the receipt and sufficiency of which is hereby acknowledged, and the further consideration of the agreement to pay by Grantees, according to the terms thereof, all principal and interest now remaining unpaid on that one (1) certain promissory note in the original principal sum of TWENTY SIX MILLION AND NO

(26,000,000.00) DOLLARS, dated February 5, 2023, executed by BACK IN POWER MINISTRIES, and payable to the order of Gertrud White, Individually and as Independent Executrix of the Estate of Milda Williams Cheek, Deceased and secured by vendor's lien retained in deed of even date therewith, recorded in Volume 2981, Page 823 of the Land Records of Cass County, Missouri, and being additionally secured by a Deed of Trust of even date therewith. Grantees assume and promise to keep and perform all the covenants and obligations of the Grantors named in said Deed of Trust, have GRANTED, SOLD and CONVEYED, and by these presents do GRANT, SELL, and CONVEY unto Grantees, all the following described real property in Cass County, Missouri, to wit:

All that certain lot, tract, or parcel of land situated within the corporate limits of the City of Kansas City, --------------- County, Missouri, and known as Lot No. Twenty-one (21) of the E. E. Griffin re-subdivision of a part of Block No. 234 of the City of Kansas City, ------, County, Missouri, as shown by a plat thereof approved by the City Plan Commission of the City of Kansas City on April 4, 1946, and recorded in the Deed Records of Cass County, Missouri, to which reference is here made for all purposes.

This conveyance is made and accepted subject to all and singular the restrictions, zoning laws, regulations, and enactments of municipal or other governmental authorities, mineral reservations, and royalties conditions, easements, and covenants, if any, applicable to and enforceable against the above-described property as reflected by the records of the County Clerk of the county in which the above-described property is located TO HAVE AND TO HOLD the above-described premises together with all and singular the rights and appurtenances thereto in anywise belonging unto the said Grantees, their heirs and assigns forever.

Grantors do hereby bind their heirs, executors, and administrators to warrant and forever defend, all and singular, the said premises unto said Grantees, their heirs, and assigns, against every person whomsoever lawfully claiming or to claim the same or any part thereof.

Taxes for the current year have been prorated and are assumed by Grantees.

But it is expressly agreed that the vendor's lien, as well as the superior title in and to the above-described premises, is retained against the above-described property, premises, and improvements until the above-described note and all interest thereon are full paid according to the face, tenor, effect, and reading thereof, when this deed shall become absolute, and, in the event of default in the payment of said not so assumed (or default in any covenant or condition of any instrument securing the payment of said note so assumed), the Grantors herein shall have the right and privilege of foreclosing the vendor's lien reserved in their favor herein.

EXECUTED this 28th day of April 2023

BACK.IN POWER MINISTRIES

By: _____

ROBERT D. SMITH, President

By: _____

BARBARA MILAM, Secretary/Treasurer

The Bible Deed.

Before I begin to explain, I must take a praise break and say, "Praise God!" For those who have not received the revelation, just hold on a minute, and I will explain. God has given us a deed of a **SPECIALITIES** nature in the word of scripture. I call it the **Bible Deed**. I do so because, for all practical purposes, it fits the criteria for a written legal description of the spiritual promises that God has given to his children. Traditionally and under the law, to be valid and enforceable, a deed must fulfill several requirements.

- First, it must be executed as a deed under the rule of law.
- It is an instrument of conveyance in that it conveys some privilege or thing to someone using the word *hereby* or some other phrases to indicate a gift.
- The grantor must have the legal ability to grant the possession or privilege.

- The grantee must have the legal capacity to receive it.
- It must be executed by the grantor in the presence of the prescribed number of witnesses, known as instrumentary witnesses. (This is known as being in **solemn form**).
- A seal must be affixed to it. Affixing seals made persons' parties to the deed.
- It must be delivered to (**delivery**) and accepted by the grantee (**acceptance**).
- It should be properly acknowledged before a competent officer.

The Spiritual Deed of Promise let us deal with each item separately and relate it to the spiritual deed of promise:

It must be executed under the rule of law. The Bible deed, in order to be valid and convey ownership, rights, and obligations, must be executed under the rule of law. The first covenant or contract that we refer to in Christendom is called the Old Testament. The word testament has a particular meaning and should be noted. A more accurate word for this definition would be a covenant. A covenant is a word that signifies "a disposition of property by will or otherwise." In its use in the Septuagint, it is the rendering of a Hebrew word meaning a "covenant or agreement (from a verb signifying "to cut or divide"). This was in allusion to a sacrificial custom in connection with "covenant-making."

In Genesis, the fifteenth chapter, when Abram made a covenant with the Lord concerning his seed, God gave him assurance that his seed would multiply as the stars of the sky.

Though Abram believed in the Lord and God counted it to him for righteousness, still he asked a question of the Lord, "...whereby shall I know that I shall inherit it?" The Lord spoke to him and gave assurance through a covenant. He said, *"Take me a heifer of three years old, and a she goat of three years old, a ram of three years old, and each piece one against another..."* This is in contradiction to the English word "covenant," which has a more literal meaning of coming together which signifies a mutual undertaking between two parties or more, each binding himself to fulfill obligations. It mostly signifies an obligation undertaken by a single person. In Galatians 3:17, it is used as an alternative to a **promise.** *"And this I say, that the covenant, that was confirmed before of God in Christ, the law, which was four hundred and thirty years after, cannot disannul, that it should make the **promise** of none effect."* The promise to Abraham in this text is called a covenant. They are used interchangeably. So, the New Testament's use of the word leans toward **promises** or undertaking. "Now unto Abraham and his seed were the **promises** made..." Galatians 3:16a. *"That the blessings of Abraham might come on the Gentiles through Jesus Christ; that we might receive the promise of the Spirit through faith."*

Paul goes to great lengths to prove to law-oriented Christians that The New Testament fulfills the criteria of the law of the Old Testament. As I have cited in the previous paragraph, the promise was given to Abraham four hundred and thirty years before the institution of the Jewish Law. Furthermore, he denounces justification under Jewish law by saying,

"For as many as are of the works of the law are under the curse: for it is written, Cursed is every one that continueth not in all things which are written in the book of the law to do them. But that no man is justified by the law in the sight of God is evident: for, The just shall live by faith. And the law is not of faith: but the man that doeth them shall live in them. Christ hath redeemed us from the curse of the law, being made a curse for us: for it is written, Cursed is every one that hangeth on a tree:" Galatians 3:10-13.

To further explain, Paul writes, *"Is the law then against the promises of God? God forbid: for if there had been a law given which could have given life, verily righteousness should have been by the law. But the scripture hath concluded all under sin, that the promise by faith of Jesus Christ might be given to them that believe. But before faith came, we were kept under the law, shut up unto the faith which should afterward be revealed. Wherefore the law was our schoolmaster to bring us unto Christ, that we might be justified by faith. But after that faith is come, we are no longer under a schoolmaster. For ye are all the children of God by faith in Christ Jesus. Galatians 3:21-26.* So, Christ satisfied the rule of law by the **law of faith** that brings redemption from the book of the Jewish law. Therefore, the first test of a Bible deed of spiritual promise is met.

Secondly, it is an instrument of conveyance in that it conveys some privilege or thing to someone using the word <u>hereby</u> or some other phrases to indicate a *gift*.

And he that keepeth his commandments dwelleth in him, and he in him. And hereby we know that he abideth in us, by the Spirit which he hath given us. I John 3:24

Hereby know we that we dwell in him, and he in us, because he hath given us of his Spirit I John 4:13.

These are three examples of the use of the word hereby in scripture that conveys some privilege and indicates a gift. According to law, let every word be established with two or three witnesses. The first privilege cited by Joshua is that of a *living God*, who marches with them. Unlike the pagan gods, the living God is able to perform mighty acts of warfare, giving them victory over their enemies and protection within their inheritance. Much can be said about a living God who has risen. This contrasts with those who are assumed to be gods but remain in the grave or have been fashioned with the hands of men. However, that will be reserved for another time.

The last two scriptures deal with the privilege of *habitation* with God through the Spirit of God that He has given us. Habitation is a word in Hebrew (yasab) which means "to dwell, sit, abide, inhabit, remain, abide. Yasab is sometimes combined with other words to form expressions in common usage. For example, *"When he sitteth upon the throne of his kingdom"* (Deut. 17:18: *And it shall be when he sitteth upon the throne of his kingdom,* and I Kings 1:13: *"… and he shall sit upon my throne…"*17,24) carries the meaning "begins to reign." "To sit in the gate" means "to hold court" or "to decide a case," as in Ruth 4:1-2: "Then went Boaz up to the gate, and sat him down there: and behold, the kinsman of whom Boaz spake came by; unto whom he said, Ho, such a one! Turn aside, sit down here. And he turned aside and sat down. And he took the ten men of the elders of the city and said Sit ye down here. And they sat down". Therefore, God **hereby** becomes the ruling force in your life through the spirit and holds court on whatever the case may be against you. He has your docket number and understands the case thoroughly but will judge with mercy and grace. Isaiah 54:17 gives us the verdict in the case, *"No weapon that is formed against thee shall prosper; and every tongue that shall rise against thee in judgment thou shalt condemn. This is the heritage of the servants of the LORD, and their righteousness is of me, saith the Lord."* Hereby, we have assurance through the promises of God that he is both the ruler and the judge of our lives. When God begins and continues to rule and judge our lives, the course of our destiny will be determined with certain assurance.

The second aspect of this requirement deals with the **gift.** One of my favorite scriptures dealing with the gift and concept of the grantor's giving references the **gift** of salvation as found in Ephesians 2:8, "For by grace are ye saved through faith; and that not of yourselves: it is the **gift** of God:" Gift in the Greek has several meanings. The first word, *doron* is interpreted as "to give," and used in relationship to gifts presented as an expression of honor or a present given for mutual celebration of an occasion as in offering. Dorea denotes a "free gift," stressing its gratuitous character. In the New Testament, it is always used as a spiritual or supernatural gift as in Acts 2:38, "the gift of the Holy Ghost". Doma lends greater stress to the character of the gift rather than to its beneficent nature, as in Matthew 7:11, "If ye then, being evil, know how to give good gifts unto your children, how much more shall your Father which is in heaven give good things to them that ask him." Charisma is "a gift" of grace, a gift involving grace which is translated (unmerited favor) on the part of God as the donor for gift and giving.

Notice the correlation of the English word, **donor,** to the Greek definitions. Donor is the English word for gifts and giving. He is the donor (giver) of all good and perfect gifts to the children of men and we are the recipients of his grace.

Let us move to the third qualification of the Bible Deed to see if it meets the criteria; the **grantor must have the legal ability to grant the possession or privilege.**

The grantor and the donor are similar in meaning. A grantor is one who contributes, donates, or conveys property. He or she allows or agrees to the dispersing of that gift by whatever terms have been agreed upon. As we have mentioned earlier, the terms can be either conditional or unconditional. However, a donor is usually the giver of gifts from an unconditional position. To meet the requirements of a legal deed, the Bible Deed must show *legal ability* on the part of the grantor to permit the dispersing of the property. The grantor must have legal ownership.

That appears to be a given in the case of the God of the whole earth. After all, "The earth is the LORD's and the fullness thereof; the world, and they that dwell therein." Psalms 24:1. "Of old hath thou laid the foundation of the earth: and the heavens are the work of thy hands." Psalms 102: 25. It is a solid case with bonafide evidence. God created the earth with the works of his hands. It and all its fullness and all the habitation of those who live in its domain belongs to him.

Where, then, is the problem? The problem lies in the covenant agreement that God made with Adam. He gave humanity dominion over His creation. "And God said, Let us make man in our image, after our likeness: and let them have dominion over the fish of the sea, and over the fowl of the air, and over the cattle, and over all the earth, and over every creeping thing that creepeth upon the earth. And God blessed them, and God said unto them, Be fruitful, and multiply, and replenish the earth, and subdue it: and have dominion over the fish of the sea, and over the fowl of the air, and over every living thing that moveth upon the earth. Genesis 1:26-28. God's decrees and commands are clear. He decreed the dominion to humankind and then issued a command to subdue it.

The word dominion, in its verb form, implies lordship and authority. "…The kings of the Gentiles exercise lordship over them, and they that exercise lordship upon them are called benefactors. St Luke 22:25.

So, when God gave humankind lordship and authority over the creation of the earth, that domain was brought under the subjection of humanity altogether. Dominion was given to him by God. In the psalmist rhetorical question, he asked, "What is man, that thou art mindful of him? and the son of man, that thou visitest him? For thou hast made him a little lower than the angels, and hast crowned him with glory and honor.

Thou madest him to have dominion over the works of thy hands; thou hast put all things under his feet: Psalms 8:4-6. Still, the question must be asked, "What does that have to do with the legal right of ownership?"

When the Adamic covenant was established between God and Adam, a covenant that most theologians call a covenant of **innocence** in that he knew no sin, that covenant became the legal and binding agreement for ownership, rights, and obligation. Ownership included the dominion of the earth and its habitation. Rights granted included rule in a divinely appointed delegated position as the representation of God upon the earth, communion with God in that he walked and talked with God in the cool of the day (Genesis 3:8) and eternal life. The very soul of man originated from the breath of God (Gk. pneuma). Can you just imagine every few seconds experiencing the presence of the Spirit of God flowing within every fiber of your being? Every twenty-three seconds, your body being renewed with not just life but life.

All provisions were made for humankind. He had food from every tree that was both pleasant to the sight and good to eat from. He had untold riches of gold, bdellium, and onyx stone, just to name a few, and although diamonds and rubies are not mentioned, we know from geological findings that they were present also. One of the greatest riches had to be a stress-free form of employment in taking care of the Garden of Eden, molded and fashioned by the very God of the universe. The peace that he experiences in the Garden is comparable to the song writer's version when he says peace is like a river flooding his soul.

He was given a perfectly formed woman from his own DNA, a real soul mate, and a helper (Gk. lamboano), which is translated as a supporter in times of weakness and in ministry or better-translated service. In marriage, they were in communion on a spiritual, intellectual, and physical level. I know that much can be said in a negative fashion concerning Eve and her committed sin of deception. Many of those views come from men who have dealt with women who have altered their original purpose from that of Eve. I say to the brothers that it was after the fall that some of the sisters got that way. Of course, to the brothers, I say if you are looking for an Eve, find one that is a close to God as she can be and one who will stay under the covered protection of your love and as far from the serpent as she can get. Still, I give Sister Eve a vote of affirmation as the mother of all living. She was all that God said she was, and all that Adam asked for, probably more. I just know something messed with his mind enough to commit a sin with knowledge of its consequences. Eve was deceived, but Adam was not. As Forest Gump would say, "that all I have to say about that." All these privileges and rights were freely given in this covenant. (Genesis 2:7-12). I am certain that there were others, too numerous for us to know or name, that were also given, but these are the ones written in the Deed.

But there were also obligations on the part of humanity to keep the covenant. And the Lord God commanded the man saying, "Of every tree of the garden thou mayest freely eat: But of the tree of good and evil, thou shalt not eat of it: for in the day that thou eatest thereof thou shalt surely die." Genesis 2:16-17. Of course, these are **commands** (Heb. miswah) which are laws and statues given by God through divine revelation and appointed to set things right in the theocratic order of God. These were not merely suggestions. God's purpose was to set up and everlasting kingdom with the first son of God, Adam, who was made in the image and likeness of God. But the transgression of the commands shattered the kingdom, causing the prince to die and the covenant to be given to a prince of darkness.

When the covenant was broken by virtue of sin, the ownership and rights were forfeited and given to a new prince. In St John 12:31, St John 14:30, and Ephesians 2:2, he is described as Satan, the prince of this world. In II Corinthians 4:4, he is described as the god of this world. Let me emphasize little "g" but nevertheless a god with ownership and rights. These rights were affirmed and were not disputed but our Lord Jesus Christ himself. As a matter of fact, he confirmed it in the previous scriptures. The deed of ownership was legally transferred to the prince of this world.

How could it get back into the hands of mankind once again? Satan was not about to just hand it over without a fight, and he did not have to. It was legally his. He could do as he desired to do. And that he did, he filled the entire world with violence. One of his first acts of dominion was to destroy another son of God, Abel. He did this through the hands of his own brother, Cain. True to his purpose, he came to *steal, kill,* and *destroy,* in that order (St John. 10:10). He came to steal our ownership, rights, and privileges. After that, he wants to steal your purpose. *Once the purpose is stolen, there is no real life. There is only breath and motion.* It is, as the unknown poet said, dead at thirty and buried at fifty, living a physical life but devoid of true purpose. These are the kinds of lives that are filled with excess drugs and all forms of habits, drunkenness with power, perversions, and pursuits of materialism without the perspective of God. They become empty shells with no substance or hope. When hope leaves, so does life. I heard it said that a man could live several weeks without food and water, a few minutes without air, but not a second without hope. If Satan can steal your hope, he will kill your purpose and destroy your destiny. Not only will this affect you, but it will also affect those with whom God has given you charge to instruct and power to influence toward their purpose.

Recovery Through the Word of Promise

How shall we recover? How shall we receive total restoration? It will be accomplished by and through the Word of God. The Word of God, as expressed through Biblical Scriptures, is both living and Holy Spirit inspired. It is a discerner of the thought and intents of the heart. It gives us proper instructions in righteousness and enlightenment in direction. It is a lamp to our feet and a light unto our path. It brings revelation and blessings. The word is perfect and everlasting and will never fail. It gives knowledge, understanding and wisdom to the unintelligent and is the ultimate truth. It brings freedom from error and deliverance to the soul. The word is a place of shelter and hope. When the word goes forth from the mouth of God to us, it will always accomplish the purpose of God and will not return to Him void. The Word gives stability and access to all the promises of God. The word is pure and shields all who trust in it. The Word is healing and deliverance from destruction. The word of God has the creative power of Grace to manifest the lifestyle we desire.

So, let us look into the Word to find the principles of recovery and restoration. As we look, we will not be limited to contextual and descriptive writing. We will also look into the text's exegetical, typical, hermeneutical and applicational aspects to discover contemporary principles for our endeavor.

The first citing will be that of a parable of Jesus Christ himself in the New Testament, and then we will allude to the text from which our title is derived.

Get It Back

This has been the question of many who have lost faith, wealth, health, relationships, other things and maybe even purpose. How do I get it all back? How do I get back to the purpose for which I was created? How do I get back to the place of belief to be restored? Let me say, first of all, that God wants you to get everything back that you have lost. God wants you to return to your place in Him, your position, purpose, status and level of integrity. God wants you to get it all back. There is rejoicing in heaven and on earth over one who can return.

As I am writing, I feel in my spirit that this is time for your personal **"COMEBACK"**! I sincerely feel that we have entered a season of recovery. The Divine opportunity is before us; the heavens are open, alignments are taking place, and good things are ready to happen. So, position yourself for your restoration! Get ready! Align yourself with the season of restoration!

Jesus Teaches in Parables

Let us look at a parabolic teaching of Jesus Christ to exemplify this notion. Here, Jesus uses the parabolic truth to articulate a principle of gathering and recovery that is timeless and applicable, irrespective of culture, age or identity.

The truth of these teachings is self-evident. God has a vital power, and He has the omnipotent power to restore that which was lost. Furthermore, it is not God's will that what He has freely given should be taken. But let us look at some of the principles necessary to realize restoration.

St Luke 15:3-10

And he spake this parable unto them, saying, What man of you, having an hundred sheep, if he lose one of them, doth not leave the ninety and nine in the wilderness, and go after that which is lost, until he find it? And when he hath found it, he layeth it on his shoulders, rejoicing. And when he cometh home, he calleth together his friends and neighbors, saying unto them,

Rejoice with me; for I have found my sheep which was lost. I say unto you, that likewise joy shall be in heaven over one that repenteth, more than over ninety and nine just persons, which need no repentance. Either what woman having ten pieces of silver, if she lose one piece, doth not light a candle, and sweep the house, and seek diligently till she find it? And when she hath found it, she calleth her friends and her neighbors together, saying Rejoice with me; for I have found the piece which I had lost. Likewise, I say unto you there is joy in the presence of the angels of God over one sinner that repenteth.

There is much to be said about the parabolic style of teaching employed by Jesus Christ. A parable may be an extended story or a pithy statement, but it always conveys spiritual truth by comparison with familiar facts. These two parables are essentially parables of restoration. A shepherd restores his lost sheep to the fold, and a woman restores her lost coin to her treasure store. These parables are an insight into the mind of God concerning those who were being officially treated as lost for whom pharisaism held out no hope.

It also gives insight into God's attitude toward the concept of loss. There is always hope of restoration with God, as He is the God of restoration. Some have said that He is the God of second chances. While that is certainly true, He is so much more. He is the God of continual restoration, whether that is one time, two times, three times, a hundred times, thousands of times or even millions and as often as restoration is needed. He can and will restore a little or much.

Let me get out on a limb and digress to say that God is not the author of loss. Loss is inevitable. It happens to us all, but it is not of God. Pause and think about that.

The truth of the matter is that the *thief* is. Let us put that blame where it belongs. As I said in the previous chapter, the thief comes for three purposes; to steal, to kill and to destroy, but the Lord has come that we might have life and have it more abundantly. God not only wants to restore what was lost, but He also wants us to have *abundance*. That word is derived from the Greek word *hadros*, which means thick, fat, full-grown or rich. Always in the Septuagint, rich and great men chiefly use it. It is always exceeding the normal measure to indicate something above the ordinary.

Let us look at the text from a distinct perspective, which I call a *"God's perspective."*

A shepherd has one hundred sheep, and one got lost. In ancient times, near the East, the figure of the shepherd was associated with gentleness, watchfulness and concern for the sheep. The primary responsibility of the shepherd was to feed, lead and heed the flock, but it is more than that. It is an emotional element involved in the care of the sheep styled like that of a pastor caring for his parishioners.

One of the first things I have noticed concerning the shepherd in this parable is that he counted his sheep. He had to do so in order to recognize that one was lost. I really do not know his method of counting. An inexperienced shepherd would, perhaps, have counted them by ones in a single bunch of the one hundred, but I seriously doubt this method was used. It would not be the most optimal and would lead to repetitive counting. The most obvious method would be that of grouping, perhaps in groups of tens.

I just mention the number ten randomly because it is the number of ordinal perfections. By ordinal perfection, I am referring to a perfect order as it relates to God's dealing with humanity.

Mankind can never achieve perfection in an absolute manner, even with the help of God, but he can have perfection of order. The number ten is the representation of that. The normal human has ten fingers and ten toes, which is figurative of the perfection of industrial order and order of purpose.

The numerical system of man is based upon a ten-digit system that begins a new order on every tenth number. The binary mathematical system for super intelligence in the major areas of computing is based upon the system of ten also. I could go on and on to establish this point, but this is not the main purpose. Again, I want to reiterate that this number was chosen randomly to emphasize a grouping. Nevertheless, the Hebrews as well as other major cultures of the Egyptians, Greeks and Orientals of the East, were aware of this significance and practiced it readily. Even in the parable, you may notice that the quantity of hundred sheep is the multiple of ten, precisely ten times ten. The woman had ten coins. You can disseminate my use of the number ten according to your spirit, but in this writing, I believe it to be spirit inspired.

The number ten further represents the fullness and completion of God's Divine order. It represents the vastness and the availability of the Master's wealth.

In Psalms 103:2, *"Bless the Lord, O my soul and forget not all his benefits"*, the word benefits is a gimel word that represents the vastness and availability of the Master's wealth which supposes that He, our God, has all the vastness, availability and intentionality to make benefits available to us and give them to us in Divine Order. In a nutshell, it indicates that whatever you need is coming to you or, in the case of loss, is coming back to you. Everything that got away is coming back. Whenever you need it, it is coming. It is intentional, and it is established!!! God will give you provision for your destiny so that your purpose may be established. Your provision and restoration will always be found in your purpose.

There should also be notice of the number ninety-nine, which is what is represented when one is lost. Ninety-nine is the number in scriptural numerology to indicate a number for the confirmed judgment. The number of nine coins, one was lost from ten, also represents judgment. So, the loss would indicate a mere insignificant loss and a change in condition, order, and status. There is an incomplete order in each case. A loss of one caused the numerical order to change from perfection to judgment. The presence of judgment or, in this case, loss is not to be confused with the perfect plan of God.

It is beneath what God has purposed. Ninety-nine or nine is a deficit of God's order and is not a part of the aggregate purpose. Remember, I have told you that God's provision for destiny is in your purpose. Now, some may be satisfied with this loss of one, but it is not God's will, and it will always alter your purpose when you adopt an attitude of acceptance of loss. Let me just say this with all boldness, *"never be satisfied or complacent with loss on any level"*. I say that simply because many people equate loss with God in pacification without understanding. It is an error to do so. Finally, do not ponder or get bogged down by the change of status as an element of judgment. I will explain it further in detail in a later chapter.

It is also not out of the question to believe that the shepherd actually recognized the physical characteristics or the distinct sound of the missing sheep. I would think that could have been a factor also. The Good Shepherd knows each sheep by name, and the sheep recognizes the distinct voice of the shepherd. (John 10:14). This is why I believe all the sheep were not included in a bunch of one hundred. It would not have allowed the individual attention needed to know the sheep and develop individual recognition.

In the methodology of recovery, one of the major points of this parable is established and found in words, *"go after it until you find it"*. Within those words are two basic principles. Number one, you must move from your position of loss to a position of recovery. This will take a conscious effort on your part and a collaborative effort with God in the restoration process. I say that because of the misguided notion that many people advance that God will do it for you. He will not! If you make an effort, God will assist you, direct you, empower you, and sometimes intervene miraculously for you, but He will not do it until you move with determination and faith. ***You must move!***

If it wanders away, it will not return on its own volition, or if it falls away, it will not find its place on its own. God will not restore it if we are apathetic. We must be diligent and collaborative in order to experience restoration. Everything that wandered away must be pursued and reclaimed. Everything that fell must be sought after, picked up and put back into its proper place. There must be an aggressive mentality present to go after that which was lost.

God uses your will, your faith and your effort to bring restoration. He uses your eyes and your diligence to discover the loss. He uses your management skills to protect and cover because if you do not manage, you will lose. He uses your feet to pursue and recover, your hands to do the untangling, and your shoulders to bear the responsibility of full restoration.

I have spoken at length concerning the Good Shepherd, but also in this parabolic teaching is the example of a woman who lost a coin in the house from the original number of ten. There is the number ten again. Now she only has nine, which is a number that I have already explained as being beneath the order and purpose of God. So, let us gather the wisdom of her effort to recover. She lights a candle. She sweeps the house and seeks diligently until she finds it.

Before we extrapolate these principles, let us note something that may not be apparent on the surface. She is a woman. I make a note of that because much of the bible teaching in done in masculine examples. Women are mentioned few and far between its pages and in many instances, they are portrayed in subjective order or in some cases for their evil character such as Jezebel. It is not my intention to extol or explore feminism or champion misogynism. I just want to make mention of her as a woman and share some specific traits of womanhood to apply to the restoration principle.

A woman is both a receptive and reproductive vessel. She is designed that way by God. Therefore, it is in her nature to receive and reproduce that which she receives and multiply it.

Dr Myles Monroe said that if you give a woman milk, eggs, flour and sugar, she can turn it into a cake. If you give her material, she can turn it into a dress, etc. So, his warning to men was to be careful not to give woman stress and a hard time, or she can turn it into something worse, multiply it and give it back to you. I know that may be antiquated in today's society, but they are his words, not mine, and there is an element of truth worth noting.

The point of my exhortation is the reception aspect of her character. In order to manifest total restoration, you must be open to receptivity. It is one of the motivating emotions that produce the kinetic energy to go after that which is lost. If you do not believe that you will receive, you will not ask, nor will you seek or pursue. Let me interject something to help you understand the mind of God concerning reception. God says, ask and it shall be given you; seek and ye shall find; knock and it shall be opened unto you. Matthew 7:7. He says, if you have faith, you will receive whatever you pray for. Matthew 21:22. He says whatever you desire when you pray, believe that you receive them, and you shall have them. Mark 11:24. These scriptures along with a plethora of others affirm that God wants you to receive. He gives you permission to receive and the steps to follow to make it happen. Always keep your receptors open to God's will to restore so you can recover all that has been lost.

Now that your receptors are open, light a candle. Although this is contextual, it is also applicable. Lighting a candle brings illumination or revelation to the situation. Now that we have permission, we must bring revelation to the process for provision and procurement and in our case, restoration. How does a person know the will of God concerning the way to restoration? If you desire wisdom from God, all you need to do is ask. He gives wisdom through the Holy Spirit while praying in the Spirit because so many times, we do not know what to ask for. That is why we need to pray in the Spirit. He will give the knowledge, understanding and wisdom of God liberally.

She swept the whole house. To do so meant that she had to move obstacles out of the way to see more clearly the landscape of the home. Of course, the reason for moving obstacles out of the way seems apparent. On the road to recovery, there will be all kinds of hindrances as well as distractions that will pop up. Most of them will be of an emotional nature, but some will be physical and logistical. A person on the road to self-recovery and restoration cannot entangle himself or herself with the affairs of every bleeding heart (symbolically) and maintain the diligence necessary to bring personal restoration. This may sound selfish but first, "to thine own self be true". That is the instructions given on commercial flights in emergency situations. Put the air mask over your nose and mouth, breathe normally and then help minors traveling with you. You cannot help anybody else if you have fainted.

Move any obstacles of whatever type and keep on sweeping with diligence until you find your valuable thing.

In this illustration, the two instances of loss have an antithetical reaction to the person seeking to recover that which was lost. The first one is of an emotional nature with the sheep, and the latter is one that appeals to economic value with the coin. Each is important, but it appeals to a different aspect of our lives. The loss that involves relationships is of an emotional nature and the loss of finances is of economic value. They are both stressors, just of different natures. Whatever the nature, let me assure you again that God wants to bring recovery in every area of loss, both emotional and economic.

The rejoicing of friends in each case is also significant. After each recovery and restoration, the shepherd and the woman called their friends to come and rejoice with them, and they did. I do not want to miss this notable point: ***"Individual effort will bring corporate rejoicing!"*** Many people, while on the road to personal recovery and total restoration, tend to look toward others to help them get out of their situation of loss and help them recover. There are some charitable people in this world, and you may be blessed to run across a few in your lifetime. You may even befriend one or two in your life. If you are so gracefully blessed, give God the praise. You are well-favored and highly blessed! That is the exception and not the norm.

Restoration begins in the fertile mind, and when that mind is exercised with skillful courage and faith, it brings the manifestation of total restoration. In this season of recovery and restoration, in order to receive the manifestation of total restoration, *we must change our minds*. Yes, we must do it. Nobody else can. God gives us the promise and the choice, but we must put forth a diligent effort. You have the God-given power to do this. The mind, or as it is referred to in scripture, *soul*, which is the Greek word psyche, referring to intellect and will, is always shaping the fabric of reality spiritually. The soul or mind of man and the spirit of man which is from God are so closely intertwined that the spirit becomes a reservoir from the issues of the mind. What you think in your mind; what you say in your mind determines the quality of life you experience. To initiate the power of total restoration and live a life of recovered purpose, conquering mistakes and defeats, wrong choices, fear, worry, continual sickness, unhealthy relationships, poverty, historical curses and bad attitudes, you must narrow the focus of the mind and with your earnest intention speak them within your soul and with your mouth to create from the invisible currents of the soul and spirit the restoration we desire on a material plane. Then and only then are the desires of restoration realized.

The Deliverance of Restoration

Some believe true deliverance and freedom are limited to coming out of something. We have testified to it in the church service about how God brought us out. We have rejoiced about not being where we were. I do not express disapproval of that practice. It is always good and in order to praise God for the marvelous benefits He gives us.

What I want to enunciate concerning deliverance is that it not only involves coming out of something but also going into something more amazing. For if we never hear, envision, touch and possess that for the purpose which we have been ordained, we have only half of the deliverance process.

Let me cite some examples to illustrate what I call the *deliverance principle.* First, in the Old Testament, we look at the prophet Moses, who was known as the deliverer of the children of Israel. The etymology of the name Moses actually means *"drawn out".*

"… And she called his name Moses: and she said Because I drew him out of the water." Exodus 2:10.

The background behind Moses being drawn out of the river has its roots in the children of Israel sojourning into the land of Egypt under the leadership of Jacob. During a time of famine, Jacob moved there to sustain his family. Joseph had already been positioned there by the evil intent of his brothers for the good of his people that would follow. They meant it for evil, but God turned their intent into His intent and worked it out for both his good and the good of all those connected to him. What is worth mentioning is that after the famine was over, they still did not return back to the land of promise until they were forced to because of the oppression of the king of Egypt. How often do the children of God make those same mistakes? They dwell in a place of provision that God has ordained for the moment well past their season and have to be forced into God's place of promise. God's people must always be in harmony with the moving of the Spirit of God because His Spirit is like the wind, moving from one direction at this moment to another direction in a different season. As the old songwriter said, *"When the Lord gets ready, you got to move"*.

They stayed for approximately 430 years in Egypt. During that period, they were blessed and were fruitful, and increased abundantly, and multiplied and waxed exceedingly mighty and the land was filled with them. (Exodus 1:7). The king that knew Joseph died, and another king assumed the throne that did not know to give the children of God favor because of Joseph. This king, because of their growth, power and prosperity, assumed that in the event of war, these people might join with their enemies and overcome them. Therefore, he put into place a strategy of slavery and, through it, oppressed and afflicted them with the burden of taskmasters through manual labor. *"But the more they afflicted them the more that multiplied and grew. And they were grieved because of the children of Israel." (Exodus 1:12).* The scripture records this period as one in which the Egyptians made the children of Israel serve rigorously. They made their lives bitter with hard bondage, in mortar, and in brick, and in all manner of service in the field. In everything they forced them to do, it was done with severity, harshness, firmness and rigidity. Yet, it had to be done with scrupulous and thorough precision.

The next phase of their oppression took on the form of infanticide. The king commanded the midwives, Shiphrah and Puah, to kill every infant son born of the Hebrews. In spite of this, the midwives feared God and did not follow the king's command, but conversely, they saved the lives of the male children. When called into question concerning their action, they avoided the punishment of the king with a craftily designed story of the virility of the Hebrew wives delivering the children before they could get to them. Needless to say, because of the fear of God and their rightful actions, God allowed the midwives to be blessed not only with their lives and their occupation but also with houses.

Still, the determinate king ordered cruel infanticide to cast the male-born children into the river to be killed but to spare the female children alive. The logic of the king was in the protection of his kingdom. He felt that by destroying the male seed, he would have a kingdom safe from war. Nevertheless, if we look further behind this, we will see the plan of the Enemy of the Lord, Satan. He is the thief, and the thief comes to steal and to kill. He is not satisfied with stealing your freedom, your prosperity, your health and wealth, but he wants to take the very life that God has given you.

Why, though, does he want to destroy the male seed? In the male seed is procreation. If the male seed is destroyed, there will be no prolongation of culture. If the women decide to marry and bear children, they would be forced to marry into either the Egyptian culture or one of the surrounding cultures. Either way, the infanticide would turn into genocide and eradicate the entire culture. This is the tactic of the enemy (Satan) that has been used by governments to destroy the foreordained purpose of entire cultures. If he can *steal* their prosperity and *kill* their seed, then he can *destroy* their purpose.

This story, though, is an amazing story of resurrection and recovery of the property and is the seed and the purpose of the Hebrew people. The very river that was ordered to kill the male children was the river that was the vehicle to save Moses. Yes, he was placed in the river, but he was *"drawn out"* of the river by the daughter of the king. That is the same king who gave the order in the first place. It is really amazing, but God can and will reverse a situation and make it turn out for the good of both His purpose and ours.

Moses became the eventual leader of the Hebrew children and drew them out of Egypt. Nonetheless, the story does not end there. If that were so, we could say that deliverance is just coming out. Moses drew them out of Egypt but did not lead them to their promise. So, again I say that true deliverance only comes with both the drawing out of bondage and the entering into promise.

The process of deliverance has another phase. It was exemplified in his successor, Joshua. Joshua's original name was Hoshea which meant (salvation). Moses, acting under the direction of the Spirit of God, changed his name to Yeshua. The etymology of the name Joshua is translated from this Hebrew word to mean The Lord Saves or The Lord is Salvation. Salvation in Hebrew is always interpreted as deliverance. The Hebrew word for this name is the exact spelling of the name Jesus. Thus, Joshua becomes an Old Testament type of Jesus Christ. It is also used in the New Testament, where it is used in reference to Joshua. It is translated as Jesus.

The typology is clear. Yes, Moses drew the people out, but Joshua took them in. Joshua then becomes the final phase of deliverance, and that phase includes conquest and inheritance of restored promise. Moses was the typology of the law, and the law led us to Christ. On the other hand, Joshua, who is a type of Christ, leads us to freedom, conquest, inheritance and restoration. If something is to be derived from this, we must note the instructions from the book of the law of Joshua to gain revelation of the methodology of conquest and inheritance and restoration of purpose.

Please do not be fooled. Conquest, inheritance and restoration must be attained through a patient process. Within the process is embodied a procedure; then comes the provision. A process involves a methodical course of action that allows you to develop means of action that will put you on the route that you have envisioned.

I say this to dispel the notion of instant recovery and restoration. For us who have experienced the power of God, we know that He can and oftentimes does deliver instantly. It is important for us to know that salvation is instant, but sanctification always involves a process. Some people look at loss and think that it was instant and wonder why recovery cannot be as quick. The truth of the matter is loss involves a process also. It was not instant. It was also a process. I will say more concerning this in the chapter that deals with the concept of loss. For now, let me deal with the process.

For every effect, there must first be a vision. The preacher properly said it, "Where there is no vision, the people perish:" Proverbs 29:18. The theological rendering of a vision is a mental image of the written, spoken, or proclaimed word of the Lord. God's decree to Joshua explains the process of getting and implementing a vision. ***This book of the law shall not depart out of thy mouth: but thou shalt meditate therein day and night, that thou mayest observe to do according to all that is*** *written therein: for then thou shalt make thy way prosperous, and then thou shalt have good success. (Joshua 1:8).*

Let us look at one section at a time. **This book of the Law shall not depart out of thy mouth**. The book of the Law was indirectly taken from the covenant of the Law of Moses. I say indirectly because it had roots in the Mosaic law. However, this book of the laws was a collection of the laws and regulations Joshua delivered to the people. It was distinct from the Book of the Law of Moses and can be appropriately called the Book of the Law of Joshua, although it is not. Joshua saw the needs of the people and applied the mosaic principles to his generation appropriately.

This is what I term the prophetic word, revelatory word or the personal word. It is taken from the word to meet your personal needs and fulfill your unique purpose. The Greeks call this *(rhema)* which denotes that which is spoken, uttered in speech, or written. It is a statement, command, or instruction. It is distinct from *logos*, which denote the expression of thought or the philosophical word. Logos is the universal word of the message from the Lord that is delivered with His authority and made effective by His power. This word "Rhema" does not refer to the whole Bible as such, but to the individual scripture that the Spirit of God brings to our remembrance for use in time of need. In many circles of Christendom, it is called "a word". Perhaps you have heard people say I need a word from the Lord. Whether they know it or not, this is what they are referring to. Sometimes those same people want someone else to give them a word when the truth of the matter is that God wants them to spend time in the study of the logos so He can personally give them a "Rhema".

This is exactly what Joshua did. He studied the Law of Moses and got a personal word from the Lord for himself first and then the people of God and wrote it down in a book.

Since commitments of any sort are easily forgotten, Joshua memorized this important transaction in both the written word and a visible object to preserve the memory for those of the present and future generations. He erected what is called the "Holy Place", probably the Tent of Meeting, specifically for the purpose of memorization and vocal commitment to these laws.

The first area of focus was speaking the law out of your mouth on a continual basis. The exhortation was simple; speak the law of the word. This practice was one of the primary ways that the Hebrews committed the word to memory. They did so with repetitious speaking. Another benefit came from this practice that could have only been revealed by the Lord of Glory. When the speech of the "Rhema" word goes forth from the confession of the mouth, there is an alignment of mind, spirit and body with the thought of God and the personal purpose that God has for you.

To speak is also intricately connected to the word confess which is translated *yadah* in the Hebrew language. This word has a dual meaning; to confess, praise and give thanks. At first glance, these meanings do not appear to be connected. But upon closer inspection, it becomes evident that each sense profoundly illuminates and interprets the other. The idea that is put forth from these meanings is to speak forth words that are praise to God. It also overlaps in meaning with a number of other Hebrew words implying "praise" or "give thanks". Halal, from whence we get our word Hallelujah is a prime example. In many circles of Christendom, it is known as the highest praise that individual congregants and congregations can offer. It is also unique in this aspect. It is a word that transcends languages. Of the over six hundred languages spoken, it remains as one of the only words of praise that has an almost identical sound in every dialect. Thus, it is evident in yadah, to confess in praise is a recital of and thanksgiving for the mighty acts of God's deliverance.

Many people, upon hearing the word confess, immediately associate it to the negative aspect of sharing sins, whether in a congregation or to someone who is spiritual in a confidential setting. Even though sin is to be confessed, especially of the underlying nature of sin that engulfs all humankind and separates us from the Holy God. God is even to be praised for His judgments by which he awakens repentance. *Have mercy upon me, O God, according to thy lovingkindness: according unto the multitude of thy tender mercies blot out my transgressions. Wash me thoroughly from mine iniquity, and cleanse me from my sin. For I acknowledge my transgressions: and my sin is ever before me. Against thee, thee only, have I sinned, and done this evil in thy sight: that thou mightiest be justified when thou speakest, and be clear when thou judgest. Psalms 51:1-4.*

The word in the Greek language is *homologeo*, which is translated as "to speak the same thing," to agree, or on one accord as in unity. Homo is the first word that refers to man or mankind, and logeo refers to the word. So, when confession is made to God, speech is to be spoken in agreement with God. In other words, speak what God is saying. The Greek meaning also has reference to praise in speaking but more so. This word implies that confession is to be done by way of celebrating with praise or making a promise. There is much to be said about the power of praise in bringing man into agreement with God and causing the heart of man to enter into an oath of faith with God. We will, therefore, explore this subject further in the contextual chapter, encouraged by praise.

Before I leave this subject, though, allow me to explore it a bit further. The mind of God is uncovered in the book of Genesis as we do an analysis of the creative power of speech. The Genesis record declares in chapter one, "And God said…." This expression precludes all creative acts. God spoke, and the general creation followed. The Psalmist later wrote in revelatory agreement: **He spoke, and it was done; he commanded, and it stood fast".** (Psalms 33:9). The New Testament writer adds his comment: **By faith we understand that the worlds have been framed by the word of God…"** (Hebrews 11:3). This is the preface to the conclusion. Before creation can come, a speech must be uttered.

Joshua understood this truth and therefore taught the people to speak the word of the law, and thereby they would *make* their way. The English word, *make* is a creative word that brings about formulation through construction. The Hebraic word has more emphasis on how this is brought about. The word *karat,* which is the Hebrew word for make, means *"to cut"* as it relates to the formulation of a covenant. Thus, creative power was rooted in the individual cutting out something that did not previously exist.

To understand the cutting power of words of faith, we must understand that faith is a spiritual force that transcends dimensions. Faith is potent both in the terrestrial dimension as well as the celestial dimension. So, when words of faith are spoken, they act like a sword to cut out faith promises sealed in the heavens and bring them into formation in the realm of the earth. Therefore, when we speak personal or prophetic words of faith, we cut our way out to our destiny.

Let me give you a good example of this. I was in the Caribbean Islands of Trinidad/Tobago as a guest speaker at an Omni conference. After the preaching, the guest minister asked the brothers to take me to a coconut grove to get me some coconut water. It is one of the island's delicacies. Well, I immediately noticed that one of the brothers had this long knife that was something between an American butcher knife and a Mongolian sword. They called it a machete. The brother was very proficient with it as he made light of the brush that stood in our way. After finally getting to the trees, he proceeded to get the coconuts down. They were not the kind of coconuts I had seen before at the grocery market in the United States.

Without hesitance, he proceeded to cut with precision at the outer covering surrounding the coconut shell. Finally, he got to something that I recognized as coconut and cut a small hole to pour the coconut water out into a container for me to drink. The coconut water was delicious and well as energizing. It was as if I was drinking an energy drink from the supermarket, only better. However, the process that he went about to derive the drink was just as noteworthy in accordance with this point. He had to cut his way through the brush that hindered our path. Then he cut the outer husk to get to another area. Finally, he got to the intended purpose.

I see the imagery of this action as it relates to the child of God in their pursuit to get to the place of their promised restoration and recovery: they must cut their way. Furthermore, even after you get to the place, you may need to do some additional cutting in order to get the sweet taste of your promise. Cutting is the order of the day if you want to make your way prosperous and have good success in your personal destiny.

I certainly did not intend to skip past a few additional steps toward our prosperity and success in life. So, allow me to go back and look at another directive of Joshua. *"But thou shalt meditate therein day and night".* The word meditate for the Christian seems to be a foreign term because many Christians relate the term to Eastern religions like Buddhism, Hinduism, Jewish Kabbalahism, Islamic Sufism or Taoism. Conversely, the words meditate stem from the Latin root meditatum, i.e., to ponder. In the Old Testament *haga* (Hebrew), means to sigh or murmur, but also to meditate, as in the case of the story of Hannah. *"Now Hannah, she spake in her heart; only her lips moved, but her voice was not heard: therefore Eli thought she had been drunken. And Eli said to her, How long wilt thou be drunken? put away thy wine from thee. And Hannah answered and said, No, my lord, I am a woman of a sorrowful spirit: I have drunk neither wine not strong drink, but have poured out my soul before the Lord".* When the Hebrew Bible was translated into Greek, *haga* became the Greek *melete*. The Latin Bible then translated *haga/melete* into meditatio, from which we derive the modern use of the term meditation.

Consequently, the word has a more contemporary use that is parallel to the term contemplation in Christianity. Jean L. Kristeller (2010). Ruth A. Baer and Kelly G. Wilson. ed. described meditation as "Spiritual engagement as a mechanism of change in mindfulness – and acceptance–based therapies". Nonetheless, meditation has a deeper meaning. In I Timothy 4:15, the use of the word has reference to "being diligent in". *"Meditate upon these things; give thyself wholly to them: for in doing this thou shalt both save thyself, and them that hear thee".* Meditate; be diligent with meticulous, painstaking effort. To understand this kind of pondering, let me give a few adjectives to describe the thought process. It is a careful, detailed, precise and thorough pondering and contemplation of the spirit within man that is done day and night in repetition that leads to *observing*.

Before I explain my observation, I want to give further clarity to 'meditation'. I had studied martial arts for several years. I started as the result of an injury that happened while I was playing football. My knee was injured severely when a defender put his helmet on my knee while I was coming around the end on a sweep play. I was sidelined for approximately six months and was told that my football days were over. Someone told me about this martial arts teacher who worked with people to rehabilitate and restore the flexibility of people who had been injured. He had helped people with amputated limbs, so I felt like he could help me. Needless to say, he did so to the point that I became proficient in martial arts skills. Before I knew it, I was jumping seven feet in the air, braking boards with my bare feet, breaking things with my hands and having a full range of motion with my whole body.

The way this was accomplished was through many techniques but one of the ones I remember the most was hyeongs which are Romanized as the word hyungs. Hyeong is a Korean term meaning "form" or "pattern". It is a systematic, prearranged sequence of martial techniques performed with or without a weapon as a form of interval training useful in developing mushin, proper kinetics and mental and physical fortitude. They are primarily used as a conditioning tool.

Hyeongs are also known as *moving meditations*. When they are done correctly with the proper breathing techniques and fluid motion, it brings a certain tranquility to both the mind and body. Inner strength is gained, and the balance of the body is maximized. In over one thousand published research studies, various methods of meditation have been linked to changes in metabolism, blood pressure, brain chemistry, and other bodily processes. Meditation has also been used in clinical settings as a method of stress and pain reduction. I did not have the clinical proof done in my dojo. I just know that after about six months of training, I did not have the pain in my knee, nor did I use crutches anymore. I was doing things that I had not ever been able to do even before my injury and that was proof enough for me.

In the traditional school that I trained under before I could advance to the next level, I would have to perform one hyeong at least three hundred times. It became so repetitive that I would see the movements in my sleep. The repetition not only caused me to learn mentally, but it conditioned my reflexes so that I found myself making moves about which I did not think. In most situations, I did not have the time to think about what I was going to do. I just reacted without thinking. My mind, body and spirit were acting in agreement.

However, something other than what I expected happened about two weeks prior to a match that I was to fight. Mind you, I had no idea that I was to fight this fight because when you are up and coming, you really do not know who you will be fighting. I began to have a night vision of me fighting with a Korean fighter that was much better than me and more experienced than me. At the end of the fight, though, I was the winner. This night vision happened two times in the space of two weeks. I just thought it to be a dream.

Two weeks later, though, I was in the dojo, and the match was set. A few seconds into the match and I noticed a feeling of déjà vu. I had seen it all. I knew how to defeat my opponent. The move that I had countered in my night vision I could see happening in slow motion, although both of us were at full speed. True to the vision, I ended up the victor by knockout. I should have been happy at my victory, but I was terrified. I was so afraid that I was into some kind of black art that was causing me to see visions. Little did I know that mediation is the prerequisite to visions. I sought counseling and let that be my last martial arts match. I retired soon after.

Now after many years from that experience, I was reading this passage, and the Lord spoke to me through the words of Joshua, *"You meditate that you may observe or get a vision."*

The word observe is akin to *eodis*, "sight" signifying penetration as in x-ray vision or sharpness as in the keen sight of an eagle. Metaphorically, it has reference to a mental vision. It is also strongly associated with the word look (*prosodokao*) of "to await" with "expectation" of the vision to be fulfilled. This idea is intricately connected with the idea of faith; which is derived from hearing the word of scripture and getting a mental image from that word to the point that you wait with expectation until the vision is accomplished. It is also interesting to look at the English word **provision,** which has its root in the two Latin words, *pro* and *vide*. Pro means beforehand

and vide is translated into the English word video, which means to see. These two words give us the formula for provision. If you can get a mental vision from meditating upon the prophetic promises of scripture and see with *keen sight* beforehand, and be assured with expectation, you will have success. Just a footnote, this is how the Hebrews of the Bible knew their God. He was Jehovah – Jireh, a Hebrew compound name for God, meaning the Lord, our provider.

It is recorded in words *"to do."* Of course, that directive is not an open-ended command, but it is to be *according to all that is written*. All that has been instructed thus far in this text is to bring us to the point of obedience to the command of God and the full commission of our purpose. Nothing is as important as obedience. It is obedience that brings success.

To get it back, the law had to be adhered to, and Jesus fulfilled every requirement of the law. He came in the fullness of the law. The law required a blood sacrifice for sin, and Jesus was that perfect sacrifice. There had to be a substitute in the form of the offense, and Jesus took on that form, bled and died. For the curse to be broken a man had to be hanged on a tree. He did that on the cross and took the curse of sin from humanity. Jesus Christ performed every requirement of the deed to transfer the assurance of the promises back to man. He, by himself, purged us from the guilt of sin, took back the deed from Satan and gave the promises back to man.

The covenant was God's legal instrument for the redemption of his people. Through it, he graciously bequeathed an inheritance of reconciliation with himself to those who were its qualified heirs. To become qualified, you must meet the condition of sincere faith in his promises. *"But without faith it is impossible to please him: for he that cometh to God must believe that he is a rewarder of them that diligently seek him". Hebrews 11:6.* The instrument of redemption or deed of redemption was first revealed in Eden to a fallen Adam. Adam, he said, *"And I will put enmity between thee and the woman, and between thy seed and her seed; it shall bruise thy head, and thou shalt bruise his heel. Genesis 3:15.*

It was confirmed to Noah. *And I, behold, I establish my covenant with you, and with your seed after you;"* Genesis 9:9. It was confirmed to Abraham and to his seed for everlasting generations. *Even the covenant which he made with Abraham, and of his oath unto Isaac; And hath confirmed the same to Jacob for a law, and to Israel for an everlasting covenant,"-*

I Chronicles 16:16,17

Its ultimate accomplishment depended upon the death of Jesus Christ, the divine testator. He died for us all and thus gave us over seven thousand seven hundred relevant promises of ownership, rights and obligations written in the Bible Deed. We have now received The GRANTEES from the GRANTOR, JESUS CHRIST.

It is filled with the promises of assurances of the word of the Testator:

In the beginning was the word and the word was with God and the word was God. John 1:1 And the word was made flesh and dwelt among us. 1:14 All scripture is given by inspiration of God, and is profitable for doctrine, for reproof, for correction, for instruction in righteousness. 2Tim 3:16. Knowing this first that no prophecy of the scripture is of any private interpretation. For the prophesy came not in old time by the will of man: but holy men of God spake as they were moved by the Holy Ghost. I Peter 1:20-21

We have been given a better covenant than the previous one that has been sealed with the blood of a better covenant, and we have the seal of the Holy Ghost. We have the witness of the disciples and five hundred altogether that he rose and implemented the deed of promise to the children of faith. The power of this covenant is such that it is sufficient enough to pay off all debts incurred while living a life of sin. And the limitation of promise is double. Not only do we have life in this world, but we have life more abundantly and, in the world, to come, eternal life.

These are the promises of the Bible Deed.

Within the scripture are promised, and all the promises of God are yea and in him Amen…. II Corinthians 1:20.

With respect to the property, not only do you have rights, but you also have the legal obligation to take possession of it. To do otherwise is the actual breaking of the law.

I pray that you can echo the sentiments of my heart as you are reading, that you not only want some of the promises to be manifested, but you want them all! You not only want wealth, but you want health. You not only want the house, but you want the home. You want the bed along with a good night's sleep. You want the food and the appetite to enjoy it. You want the promises of scripture,

"...that thou mayest prosper and be in health even as thy soul prospereth" III John 2.

To some, this may appear avaricious but not according to God's will. According to the Bible deed, these are your promises; not possessing them is the breaking of the law. You are under obligation and orders of the law to possess your rights.

So where is the paradox? I sincerely believe some have lost and, at this moment, are losing. This may sound harsh and offensive, but it is a book about losers. Let me clarify that statement before vanity sets in and you throw this book out the window. I am not referring to a loser in the sense that the world uses it; referring to someone who will never be a success in life. I am referring to someone who, through the storms of life, has incurred loss through their own fault or through the fault of others or events beyond their control. More than that, though, it is about the attitude and the methodology of recovery. It explores the spiritual, emotional and even the physical state of recovery. However, I am convinced that once an individual has mastered this area, spiritual, social, psychological and financial recovery and full restoration will follow.

I speak of promises that are foreordained and destined and certain. These are spiritual and theological terms, so by now, you may have determined that this is also a book that deals with Biblical principles.

This Scripture is self-explanatory and does not necessarily need interpretation, but I will elaborate. **God has blessed us!** What an amazing statement! The word in Greek for blessed is happy, to be envied, spiritually prosperous – with life joy and satisfaction in God's favor and salvation, regardless of outward conditions). Let us deal with the first definition. God has given us happiness. Happiness, in this sense, has reference to the pleasure, gladness and cheerfulness experienced in a carnal manner. This relates to the six senses of humanity wherein we communicate with the environment around us; sight, sound, touch, taste, hearing, and smell. So, this includes the things that make us happy; the provision and protection we seek for security, the love and comfort we desire for a sense of belonging; the family for cohesion.

A Time of Loss

I spoke briefly about the loss that occurred during the pandemic. Some are even projecting a greater degree of loss even as I am writing. Some major banks have failed, and some economists are projecting a recession coming out of this inflation. This is noteworthy because, usually, these dramatic economic events are registered in undeveloped countries. However, some are saying this could be worldwide. The first major recession in 2000 - 2001 affected the European Union and the United States. The National Bureau of Economic Research (NBER), which is a private, nonprofit, nonpartisan organization charged with determining economic recessions, determined the United States economy was in recession from November 2000 to October 2001, a period of eleven months at the beginning of President George W. Bush's term in office. To complicate this recession after the September 11, 2001, attacks on the World Trade Center Towers, the Dow Jones Industrial Average suffered its worst one-day point loss and biggest one-week losses in history. The market rebounded but crashed again in the final two quarters of 2003.

With the unemployment statistics considered and defined, it would have been determined that the first recession lasted from 2001 through 2003 in the United States. During this period, entire cities, counties, and states saw their reserves depleted, so much so that business as usual was a thing of the past. Municipalities were found searching for ways to maintain their existence. Of course, in an environment such as this, individual households suffered great loss as well. Family losses of both income and possessions were recorded on every corner. With these losses, both losses of courage in a spiritual and emotional sense occurred. With that came a sense of uncertainty as well.

Foreclosures were at an all-time high in the housing industry. Stocks, 401k, and retirement accounts were completely wiped out. Unemployment nationally reached an all-time high of 10%, while various sectors of the nation registered as high as 16% unemployment.

Underemployment was also an issue as people moved from one sector of the economy to another, hoping for some semblance of compensation that would meet their needs.

Natural disasters in countries throughout the world have caused the loss of life and property and the basic necessities of living to vanish in a single day. Hurricanes, tornadoes and one hundred year and five hundred year and even one-thousand-year floods have blown away and washed away dreams. Families have been torn apart, and hopelessness and despair have replaced courage and fortitude. People were full of lack and despair.

Some economic forecasters are predicting a repeat of that era and an economic disaster for this year and the coming year if the debt ceiling is not met. Let me counter those predictions and say, "Not So." This is the time of recovery and restoration.

I turned to the Scriptures to find further principles of recovery and restoration, this time in the Old Testament. In I Samuel 30, I found a step-by-step analogy of loss and recovery. And though this analogy is contained in Old Testament writings, those things that were written afore time were written for our learning that we might have hope through patience and comfort of scriptures. All scriptures cited will be based on the King James

Version except otherwise noted.

1   *And it came to pass, when David and his men were come to Zik lag on the third day that the Amalekites had invaded the south, and Zik lag, and burned it with fire;*

2   *And had taken the women captives, that were therein: they slew not any, either great or small, but carried them away, and went on their way.*

3   *So, David and his men came to the city, and, behold, it was burned with fire; and their wives, and their sons, and their daughters, were taken captives.*

4   *Then David and the people that were with him lifted up their voice and wept, until they had no more power to weep.*

5   *And David's two wives were taken captives, Ahinoam the Jezreelitess, and Abigail the wife of Nabal the Carmelite.*

6   *And David was greatly distressed; for the people spake of stoning him, because the soul of all the people was grieved, every man for sons and for his daughters: but David encouraged himself in the Lord his God.*

7   *And David said to Abiathar the priest, Ahimelech's son, I pray thee, bring me hither the ephod. And Abiathar brought thither the ephod to David.*

8   *And David enquired at the Lord, saying, Shall I pursue after this troop? Shall I overtake them? And he answered him,*

Pursue: for thou shalt surely overtake them, and without fail recover all.

9 *So David went, he and the six hundred men that were with him and came to the brook Besor, where those that were left behind stayed.*

10 *But David pursued, he and the four hundred men: for the two hundred abode behind, which were so faint that they could not go over the brook Besor.*

11 *And they found and Egyptian in the field, and brought him to David and gave him bread, and he did eat; and they made him drink water;*

12 *And they gave him a piece of a cake of figs, and two clusters of raisins; and when he had eaten, his spirit came again to him: for he had eaten no bread, nor drunk any water, three days and three nights.*

13 *And David said unto him, To whom belongeth thou? and whence art thou? And he said, I am a young man of Egypt, servant to an Amalekite; and my master left me, because three days agone I fell sick.*

14 *We made an invasion upon the south of the Cherethites, and upon the coast which belongeth to Judah, and upon the south of Caleb; and we burned Zik lag with fire.*

15 *And David said to him, Canst thou bring me down to this company? And he said Swear unto me by God, that thou will neither kill me, nor deliver me into the hands of my master, and I will bring thee down to this company.*

16 *And when he had brought him down, behold they were spread abroad upon all the earth, eating and drinking, and*

> *dancing, because of all the greats spoil that they had taken out of the land of the Philistines and out of the land of Judah.*
> 17 *And David smote them from the twilight unto the even of the next day: and there escaped not a man of them, save four hundred young men, which rode upon camels, and fled.*
> 18 *And David recovered all that the Amalekites had carried away: and David rescued his two wives.*
> 19 *And there was nothing lacking to them, neither small nor great, neither sons nor daughters, neither spoil, nor any thing that they had taken to them: David recovered all.*
> 20 *And David took all the flocks and the herds, which they drave before the other cattle, and said, This is David's spoil.*

How Did I Get into This Mess, and How Do I Get Out?

The first question many people ask when a loss occurs is why this happens to them. That may seem appropriate at the time, but a better question might be how it happened, and an even better question may be, "How do I get out of this mess?"

To embrace the first notion is to alleviate the possibility and probability that a sovereign God is in control. Furthermore, it emphasizes non-productive thoughts. If the question were answered and the intricacies were known, it still would not aid in future prevention. So, I will focus on "HOW" for that specific reason.

God is sovereign. Nevertheless, to say that loss is God's will like so many of us in the church world have come to believe, I simply cannot accept. True enough, life is filled with uncertainties, but not to an omniscient God who knows all. Yes, he knows that things will happen, when they will happen and why they will happen but that does not excuse liability on our part and impose responsibility for everything that happens to us upon God. If we discover how loss happens, then we can prevent it in many cases.

Concerning the omniscient knowledge of God, David the Psalmist wrote:

O Lord, thou hast searched me, and known me. Thou knowest my downsitting and mine uprising, thou understandest my thought afar off. Thou compassest my path and my lying down, and art acquainted with all my ways. For there is not a word in my tongue, but, lo, O Lord, thou knowest it altogether. Thou hast beset me behind and before, and laid thine hand upon me. Such knowledge is too wonderful for me; it is high, I cannot attain unto it. Whither shall I go from thy spirit? Or whither shall I flee from thy presence? If I ascend up into the heaven, thou art there: if I make my bed in hell, behold, thou art there. If I take the wings of the morning, and dwell in the uttermost parts of the sea; Even there shall thy hand lead me, and thy right hand shall hold me. If I say, Surely the darkness shall cover me; even the night shall be light about me. Yea, the darkness hideth not from thee; but the night shine Yea, the darkness hideth not from thee; but the night shineth as the day: the darkness and the light are both alike to thee. For thou has possessed my reins: thou hast covered me in my mother's womb. I will praise thee; for I am fearfully and wonderfully made; marvelous are thy works; and that my soul knoweth right well. My substance was not hid from thee, when I was made in secret, and curiously wrought in the lowest part of the earth. Thine eyes did see my substance, yet being unperfect; and in thy book all my members were written, which in continuance were fashioned, when as yet there was none of them. How precious also are thy thoughts unto me, O God! how great is the sum of them! If I should count them, they are more in number than the sand: when I awake, I am still with thee.

God has perfect and intimate knowledge of us and all the motions and actions of our inward and outward being. No matter how private or how well-kept our secrets may seem to be, our God still knows it all. God knows where we are and what we are doing every second, minute and hour of the day. He knows all that has been entrusted into our hands. God knows the country, state, city and address that we reside in and the home that we live in. He knows the bed that we sleep in and the dreams we have while asleep, even the ones we cannot remember. He knows when we go to sleep and when we wake up. He knows our spiritual slumber and physical weakness as well as our moral strengths and integrity. He knows when we come home and how we behave before our family members. He knows not only the words that are spoken but also every imagination that enters the mind and settles into our hearts. He understands our thoughts while we are thinking them and even before they enter our minds. He has a bird's eye view from heaven where He is able to see into the depths of the heart and know the pondering of the emotions. Concerning speech, he knows every word spoken in both good and vain. He is able to comprehend the whole weight of those words and the thoughts behind them that are not revealed in speaking.

He is omniscient and also omnipresence. Therefore, we are unable to elude him by flight from city to city or even to another country. It is ludicrous to think that just because we cannot see God that He cannot see us. If you turn to the right, He is there, or to the left, He is facing us. Even if we go to the most remote place on this planet, above this planet or beneath this planet, He is still there. There is no distance, time, dimension or realm that is beyond his travel. Even after we are removed from the sight of the living, He is still with us.

No veil can hide us from God's eye, nor can the darkness of night hide us from his x-ray and night vision. No hypocritical mask or disguise, no matter how spurious, can deter the Lord God from knowing the true essence of their being. He causes all to appear before him in perfect light.

God made us. Since that is so, He knows all the workings of us. He covered us in the womb of our mothers and made us in secret. I know no person who has ever seen the soul or the spirit of man, yet our God is the one who made them both. Of all the inventions of man, no scientist has ever invented a man from the substance of the earth. We are fearfully and wonderfully, and intricately formed by eternal wisdom.

Moreover, we were formed according to the written plan of God that was established before there was even a hint of substance concerning us.

In view of all this, I must ask a few simple questions. Do you think that God was aware of the foreclosure of our house or the eviction from our apartment? Did God know of our bankruptcy? Did our God know about the death of our loved one? Did He see the marriage not working out and ending in divorce? Did He see the children becoming addicted to drugs and alcohol? Did He see the son turning against the mother or the daughter being rejected by the mother? Did He see the church that He told you to start being disbanded after forty years of labor? The answer to all of these questions is yes. He knew. He knew the exact date. He also knew why and, more importantly, the process that led to these actions.

As I alluded to in the opening paragraph of this chapter, we often ask the wrong questions. As a result of asking the wrong questions, we get the wrong answers. Many of the questions of why may never be answered until we see our God face to face. Some things will only be reserved for the knowledge of the all-wise God. Some things are the direct result of the sovereignty of Almighty God, but some things are the result of cause and effect. I make no attempt to unravel the mind of God concerning those things that are reserved for Him and Him alone. My attempt is to deal with those things that we have willingly given space and permission to the enemy to come in and rob us and afterward learn how to recover from those losses once they occur.

So, again I ask the question, "How?" As in the case of David, he completed a series of actions that can be looked upon with hindsight and evaluated to render prevention for the studious learner. The first thing that I would like to note is that David and his men left their property and their families *uncovered* and *unprotected*. We will see later that he institutes a law of David concerning this very thing so as to avert any future loss. Therein is the first answer to the question of how this could have happened and what could be done to prevent it.

When God allows you to be steward over property, possession of any kind and leader of a family, you must keep all that pertains to you covered. What do I mean by this? The shepherds of the East had a practice that exemplified this principle. They would cover the sheep with olive oil to prevent the flies of the field from lighting upon them. Not only would the flies light on them, but they would, as the shepherd would say, *blow* on them and create sores. Blowing refers to the flies finding open wounds on the sheep and secreting their own fluids into the wound of the sheep, thereby contaminating the wound and affecting the health of the sheep. The olive oil would provide a covering that would expel the flies and protect the sheep.

The inference is clear in this practice, and it has application to those who would protect their family. You must keep them *covered*. Let us look at the applications. Sheep are often referred to as the family of God. The field would be the place of their sojourning in as much as the shepherds were considered nomadic. The Shepherds are those who lead and protect them. Flies are often thought to be evil forces of the air. Beelzebub is considered to be the Lord of the Flies in some cultures. The method of covering was olive oil which represents the anointing of the Spirit of God. This is my application of this practice. As the children of the family of God sojourn through this world, they will encounter oppositional forces that will endeavor to take advantage of their wounds. These flies or demonic forces will exude all kinds of negativity toward them and in them in order to weaken, sicken and even kill when possible. In spite of these efforts on the part of *the flies,* God's people must always remain covered with the covering of the Spirit of God, His anointing and His blood.

The initial covering begins with faith in God and water baptism into Christ:

"And brought them out, and said, Sirs, what must I do to be saved? And they said, Believe on the Lord Jesus Christ, and thou shalt be saved, and thy house. And they spake unto him the word of the Lord, and to all that were in his house. And he took them the same hour of the night, and washed their stripes; and was baptized, he and all his, straightway". Acts 16:30-33.

"Know ye not, that so many of us as were baptized into Jesus Christ were baptized into his death? Therefore we are buried with him by baptism into death: that like as Christ was

raised up from the dead by the glory of the Father, even so we also should walk in newness of life". Romans 6:3-4

"That he might sanctify and cleanse it with the washing of the water by the word," Ephesians 5:26

Not by works of righteousness which we have done, but according to his mercy he saved us, by the washing or regeneration, and renewing of the Holy Ghost; Titus 3:5

If we confess our sins, he is faithful and just to forgive us our sins, and to cleanse us from all unrighteousness. I John 1:9

In every phase of our lives, we must stay covered. We can gather people of similar faith with us in agreement to pray with us to keep us covered. We can also form covenants of accountability through friendship and mentorship to help us stay covered.

Nevertheless, the end result boils down to us taking the personal responsibility of being covered each and every day with the protective armor of God over us. Paul describes the covering process this way:

"Finally, my brethren, be strong in the Lord, and in the power of his might. Put on the whole armour of God, that ye may be able to stand against the wiles of the devil. For we wrestle not against flesh and blood, but against principalities, against powers, against the rulers of the darkness of this world, against spiritual wickedness in high places. Wherefore take unto you the whole armour of God, that ye may be able to withstand in the evil day, and having done all, to stand. Stand

therefore, having your loins girt about with truth, and having on the breastplate of righteousness; And your feet shod with the preparation of the gospel of peace; Above all, taking the shield of faith, wherewith ye shall be able to quench all the fiery darts of the wicked. And take the helmet of salvation. And the sword of the Spirit, which is the word of God: Praying always with all prayer and supplication in the Spirit, and watching thereunto with all perseverance and supplication for all saints;" Ephesians 6:10-18

I believe that every child of God should cover themselves daily in prayer before going out into the field of the world, as a warrior would cover himself before the battle. In practical application, it can be done in this way.

- Girt up your loins. The area referring to loins is the center of the body and the most vulnerable for the male warrior. There are sensitive pressure points located in this area that require additional protection. It is no wonder that this area is addressed first. As in the case of the natural man, so it is in the case of the spiritual man. The center of man is described in the Hebrew culture as the soul. Of course, the soul is synonymous with the word (Gk. *psuche*), which denotes the breath of life. It refers to the natural life of the body, the seat of the sentient element in man by which he perceives, reflects, feels and desires. It is the seat of his personality, his intellect and his will. The soul is the reservoir of both the body and the spirit of man. Therefore, it is important how we safeguard the soul. If the residue of the reflections of the body is poured into the soul and that residue is of a carnal nature, then the soul will be, tainted, bringing the state of that man to ruin. Then again, if the soul is fed from the unction of the Spirit, that man will become a spiritual man empowered with spiritual gifts and holy character that will bring glory to God.

1. The soul, therefore, must be clothed with truth. Truth, in the eyes of many, is relative to perception, as well as the environment. This is called perceived truth. I heard a minister recounting his experience in a foreign country where he saw men walking hand in hand. This was a customary practice in their culture and not considered strange. He, being from the States and from the urban portion of his city, considered this action inappropriate and was uncomfortable. He actually joked that each time his guide would extend his hand to take him, he was inclined to put his hand in his pocket or scratch his head to avoid holding another man's hand while walking. The truth to him was not the truth to his foreign brothers.

2. There is an imagined truth. This is a truth that seems true because of your experiences, but actually is not. In his book, **Good to Great**, Jim Collins recounts the story of a woman in one of his audiences. He called this woman from the audience for a demonstration. To complete the demonstration, he brought a chair and asked the woman to sit in it. He reassured her that no matter what happens in

the next few seconds, he would not harm her in the demonstration. In an effort to reassure her, he repeated the endorsement, "I will not harm you." The woman in affirmation, agreed with the assurance. Then, without notice, he yelled loudly into her ear. The response of the woman was unexpected. She began to cry. Mr. Collins questioned the woman concerning her response why she cried, and she replied, "You scared me". Mr. Collins insisted that he assured her that he would not harm her and had witnesses to that assurance. Then he further proceeded to explain that the normal response was to jump in surprise but not to cry. He asked her again concerning her response. She told him of the time when she was a little girl, sitting at the table that her father would yell at her for not eating her food. Mr. Collins asked her was she at a table. She replied, "No". He asked her if she saw food. Again, she replied, "No". He asked her if he was her father, and again, she replied, "No". The essence of this story's meaning lies in her imagination. Because of her past experiences, she imagined a scenario that was not actually taking place. It was only an imagined truth.

3. The truth that our soul must be girded with is the real truth, not perceived truth or imagined truth. The most reliable definition of truth is found in the scripture, *"Jesus saith unto him, I am the way, the truth, and the life…" John 14:6*. Only Jesus Christ is the real truth. When we become acquainted with that truth, it brings freedom in every area of our lives. *"And ye shall know the truth, and the truth*

shall make you free" John 8:34. For that reason, when we gird or wrap tightly our loins; we must do so with his words, his character and his truth.

4. A final note on the girding ourselves with truth should be added. We have already mentioned the mid-section of mankind and its vulnerability as well as its susceptibility. Allow me as the young people say, "to be real". One of weakness of the modern-day church has to do with the area of the loins. It is aptly named sexual sins. We have been hearing about the downfall of ministers and great ministries because men and women in the capacity of leadership have not girded themselves with truth. No one needs to have a degree in theology to recognize the effects of sexual sins. These sins will bring the honorable down to a piece of bread. They will rob him of his wealth and dignity. They will bring reproach that will never be wiped away. The offender will lose, maybe even his life. (Proverbs 6:25-33).

- Put on the breastplate of righteousness. Once more we consider another piece of armor that covers a vital part of the body, the torso. Within this area are the most vital organs within the body with the exception of the brain and that will be covered shortly. The heart, the lungs, liver, pancreas, stomach, kidneys, large and small intestines, etc. I include the lower area of the torso because the breastplate of the time was extended to protect these areas as well. Even a small wound that would penetrate one of these areas could prove to be a mortal wound.

1. Concerning the Spiritual aspect of this, let us focus upon the heart first as the center of their actions rather than their heart. If the adverse is true, then people get caught up in stirred up feelings that eventually enter the heart. As you know, this can be catastrophic. A term has been coined "Hopeless Romantic" to indicate that this type of person is idealistic rather than realistic. He or she sees things the way they want them to be rather than how they really are. Their actions follow this pattern even when things are right before them, they are unable to see or feel any different. They are dream oriented and starry eyed, living in a fantasy world hopefully believing that one day they will change their frog into a prince or awaken their sleeping beauty. At all times and in situations that appear to be amorous, still, we must protect our emotions from becoming quixotic with the quality of righteousness. Righteousness is the quality of exemplifying moral rectitude and epitomizing the character of being right and just.

- Shod your feet with *peace.* Footwear may not seem important to the casual reader but ask any fighter the importance of proper footwear. The primary importance of footwear is mobility. The warrior must be agile. We have all heard the term 'light-footed'. It indicates that the warrior is nimble and also graceful. For the warrior, balance is imperative. As long as he is on his feet, he has a chance of winning, but when he is on the ground, the chances diminish. There are fighting positions that most martial artists recognize. For every maneuver, there is a stance to acclimatize it. The masterful warrior learns all of these prerequisites before battle and uses them when the time is right.

1. A propos to the spiritual suggests that the gospel of peace is the guiding and mobile force that wins the battle for us in the trenches. These two words, gospel and peace are related closely in this exhortation. The gospel is, of course, the good news of the death, burial and resurrection of our Lord and Savior, Jesus Christ. It is the proclamation of how these actions on the part of our Savior brought peace in the heaven and glory to God in the highest. *"Blessed be the King that cometh in the name of the Lord: peace in heaven, and glory in the highest" St Luke 19:38.* What none of the Old Testament multiple peace offering could do, Jesus Christ did in one offering of himself. No believing Christian ever has to live under the shadow of condemnation any longer. Now, that we have been justified by faith, we have peace with God through the Lord Jesus Christ. (Romans 5:1). The paraphrasing is mine. *"And the peace of God, which passeth all understanding, shall keep your hearts and minds through Christ Jesus." Philippians' 4:7.*

We give God Praise for peace!

- Take the shield of *faith.* An additional piece of defensive armor is employed. Although this shield of faith is in fact a defensive weapon, it is additionally impermanent as the other weaponry mentioned so far. Thus, it can and does protect many areas of the body with what I designate as a double protection or covering. It was specifically used for the protection from fiery darts and arrows of the enemy. In the Grecian army, the entire fighting force would huddle under their shield to form a tortoise position for protection. An alternative use of the shield was to use it as a weapon. Some edges of shields were fashioned with sharp offensive weaponry to kill the enemy and others were made of metals that could be used as blunt force weapons when swords were knocked away in battle.

1. The spiritual connotation of faith is applicable in so many areas that we will only mention a few in this segment and include others in the segment that deals with faith in connection to praise. The notable thing worth mentioning here is that faith totally extinguishes the fire of the enemy. Most shields had some form of retardant placed upon the shield and soaked into the shield because most were fashioned from wood and covered with metal edges. Some were entirely made of metal but were not generally used in fighting but for royal occasions. So, when the fiery arrows or darts connected with the shield, the shield would function as a retardant. What a wonderful picture of battle with the enemy. He shoots his best arrows of fire, and the shield of faith extinguishes it upon contact. When faith is on display, that is the way it is discernible. It may be obscure

until the battle gets hot, but when necessity occurs, it is there to snuff out all the fire of the devil.

- Take the helmet of salvation. It was as if by intent that Paul saves the most important defensive piece of armor for the last as it to make a note of it. The head is the most important part of the body. In it, the brain functions. Eyesight and hearing come forth from the head. Speech, smell, and taste are all from the head. Because the helmets of warriors were so restrictive, so much so that often only small portions were left open for sight, it would be counterproductive to place it on first. These were usually made from metal and forged until hardened appropriately.

1. The spiritual nuance suggests that this piece of armor is for salvation. The word salvation is also used frequently to indicate deliverance. Hence, deliverance comes from the head or more specifically, the thoughts of the mind. *"For the weapons of our warfare are not carnal, but mighty through God to the pulling down of strong holds); Casting down imaginations, and every high thing that exalteth itself against the knowledge of God, and bringing into captivity every thought to the obedience of Christ"*. When thoughts of the mind are made subject to the obedience of Christ, who suffered to the death in obedience, deliverance will always follow.

- Take the sword of the Spirit which is the word of God. Here is primarily an offensive weapon but on occasions, were used to defend from other swords. Sword fighting usually followed a pattern of movements that were predominately offensive. The idea was to immediately remove the enemy quickly and go to the next battle. Only in cases of extreme mastery did battles last longer than a few moments.

1. Thus, the sword of the word is deliberate in its purpose. It is to totally remove the enemy from battle and render him as a defeated foe left on the battlefield to never fight in that arena again. One of the most important aspects of this weapon is that it is the word of God. This is not just the universal word of the Lord. It is the "rhema" word of the Lord. It is the personal, prophetic and applicable word that brings total annihilation to the enemy.

- All of the weaponry is appropriated by prayer. One of the ways I suggest doing this is by literally praying over each piece of the armor with supplication and intercession for both ourselves, our families and our property and then confessing and declaring the word of the Lord in each area until done. This is merely a prayer pattern. I believe that God will give each of you who undertake this endeavor of prayer covering with your own personal prayer covering, but here is a guide.

Dear Lord Jesus,

    I thank You for the privilege of family and possession. I recognize that You have given according to your sovereign authority. Thank You for allowing me to have rule and stewardship in your kingdom. Now, I come to You to do according to Your divine plan to not only keep what you have given but also to increase it. I began with me. Cover me Lord with Your blood that washes, Your anointed spirit that empowers and Your mercy that is new every morning. I put on the whole armor of God as a representative of You today in the world. I cover my loins with truth. Your word is truth. The truth shall make me free and keep me free from youthful lust and all desires that are contrary to Your word. I abstain from fornication and all uncleanness. My body is the temple of God, and I will use it for Your glory. I will not join my body to another outside of the bond of marriage. I will enjoy the wife of my youth and will not drink waters from another cistern or have fountains from my loins in the street. I will not allow the sin of adultery to shame or disgrace me and cause me ruin. I will not allow myself to get into compromising positions that could lead to error. I will stay protected at all times. I speak health and healing to this area of my body. None of the diseases that normally affect this area will come upon me. I rebuke testicular and prostate cancer and hemorrhoids. I will continually function as You created me to function, with potency and satisfaction. I am free by Your word and will walk in that freedom and integrity today to give You glory from my life.

I put on the breastplate of righteousness to cover the emotions of my heart. I have believed You and You have counted it as righteousness unto me. My righteousness will answer for me in days of accusation for I have walked upright before You, Lord. I will be rewarded and recompensed according to my righteousness. Make me to prosper because I have walked upright. Wealth and riches shall be in the house of the righteous. He leadeth me in the path of righteousness for His name's sake and I will follow this path today. The work of righteousness shall be peace; and the effect of righteousness shall be quietness and assurance forever. Let Your righteousness rain down on me this day and allow my heart to receive it and bring forth salvation. My tongue shall talk of Your righteousness all day long and I will praise You from my heart and my lips.

I speak health and healing to all my vital organs. They will function properly. I rebuke heart problems. My breathing shall be deep and bring me into a relaxed state. I am healed and healthy.

I put on the shoes of peace as I take the gospel of peace to a world in need of peace. Every place that I step today, I declare that peace will follow. My feet shall be like hinds' feet, and I will be swift to perform my purpose for today. I will walk in my high places. I will have physical balance and strength uncommon for my age. I will share peace with those who will receive me. I will be at peace even among those who are at war against me because peace is in my heart. I have great peace because my mind is stayed upon the Lord. I have the peace of God that passes all understanding and nothing shall drive away my peace.

I take the shield of faith in order to quench the fiery darts of the enemy. I will snuff out the enemy and will not be defeated in my purpose today. My faith will manifest itself for whatever victory I have need of. Today is the day of victory. I believe therefore I am. I declare and it shall be. My enemies will not rejoice over me but will be brought to shame and ruin. I will stand and remain standing when the battle is over. God is my shield and my battle ax. I will not be afraid but will be of good courage. Good things will happen today because I will trust in You.

I take the helmet of salvation to protect my mind. I will have the mind of Christ. I bring every thought captive to the knowledge of Jesus Christ. I will meditate upon the Lord and proclaim His name in praise because He is my deliverer. I will be alert and diligent. I will accomplish the task for today and will not be lacking. I am empowered to think clearly and see with Godly vision. I hear His voice clearly and speak what I hear. It is the voice of greatness and not lack. My mind shall be stayed upon Him today and I will be blessed with great favor.

I take the sword of the spirit which is the word of the Lord. I use it skillfully to defeat my enemy. Today, he will flee the word of my sword. He will be defeated in this area of my life. I am more than a conqueror. My hand shall be swift and my victory sure. Nothing shall in any wise harm me.

I pray these coverings over me and my family, my dwelling and transportation. I bless my finances and rebuke the devourer. My God shall supply all of our needs according to his riches in glory. I will receive special favor from the Lord on this day because of His loving-kindness toward me. My family shall be blessed because they are connected to me. Those who have blessed me will be blessed and those who curse me will heap upon themselves curses. All of my children will be saved and glorify God. My grandchildren will be saved. I and all that pertains to me are covered so that the enemy cannot steal anything from me. Great is our God! He is faithful to His word!

David's uncovering began well before this loss occurred as is the case of all who lose via uncovering. You just do not wake up one morning and suffer a massive loss. Loss is gradual and involves a process. Many times, this loss is actually precipitated by warning. Permit me to analyze this situation so we may learn from it.

David was anointed and appointed to be the successor of the throne of all Israel as a result of the rejection of King Saul. In the process though, he encountered resistance from Saul so much so that Saul chased him outside the boundaries of the kingdom under threat of death. This is a principle that I would like to explore further. It is a principle that I term the "Saul Syndrome". Saul discovered David in a battle with Goliath and David slayed the giant. As a result, David was brought into the palace. His exploits continued until the women singers coined a song in honor of David, saying, "Saul has killed his thousands and David has killed his ten thousands". This infuriated Saul and an evil spirit entered Saul. This spirit manifested envy, jealousy and hatred to the point that he tried to murder David.

When you are appointed and anointed for greatness in God, everybody will not be happy for you. Everybody will not support you. Some of the people that you think should help you will actually be against you. Some of your acquaintances will actually endeavor to hinder you. They are dream busters. Another term that this generation uses to describe them is "haters".

As in the case of David, this was the supreme ruler over all Israel, King Saul. He saw this man anointed of God and well favored in all the kingdom. He knew that he was rejected of the Lord and most likely knew within himself that this man would be king. I am sure that he was preparing his son, Jonathan to become king after his death and now he had to deal with David. Political maneuvering in this time was brutal and often deadly when opposed. Perhaps, the spirit within Saul was just so opposed to the spirit of David that he wanted to kill him. I am sure there was much rationale put into mind concerning David.

Nonetheless, David was God's choice. In many churches, the spoil system and nepotism are in place to the point that family and friends are considered well before other more qualified constituents. In some cases, this is racial bias where preference of race is the determinate factor for promotion. Whatever the consideration, if it is not of God and is being influenced by the Saul Syndrome, it will produce problems for not only the oppressed but also the oppressor. The kingdom of God will not be served well, and loss will occur.

David ran from the presence of Saul for fear of his life and the security of his family, his army and those others allied with him. *And David said in his heart, I shall now perish one day by the hand of Saul: there is nothing better for me than that I should speedily escape into the land of the Philistines; and Saul shall despair of me, to seek me any more in any coast of Israel: so shall I escape out of his hand And David arose , and he passed over with the six hundred men that were with him unto Achish, the son of Maoch, king of Gath. And David dwelth with Achish at Gath, he and his men every man with his household, even David with his two wives, Ahinoam the Jesreelitess, and Abigail the Carmelitess, Nabal's wife. I Samuel 27:1-4.* Though ironic as it may seem, he found solace and security among one of the primary enemies of Israel, the Philistines. He allied himself with Achish and gained favor with him. Achish gave him the town and country of Zik lag to dwell. He gained the trust of Achish and a reputation with him of being upright in integrity and good in battle. His plan was working - for now.

The law forbade alliances with the enemies of Israel and the inhabitants of the surrounding land. *Thou shalt make no covenant with them, nor with their gods. They shall not dwell in thy land, lest they make thee sin against me: for if thou serve their gods, it will surely be a snare unto thee. Exodus 23:32-33.* The idea behind this law was to keep Israel from the service of their gods, the emulation of their works and the diseases common to them. *And ye shall serve the Lord your God, and he shall bless thy bread, and thy water; and I will take sickness away from the midst of thee. Exodus 23:25.*

All things considered; I will not be too extremely critical of David in this regard. It was a case of survival. Sometimes, people of God do not always follow the rules when it comes to survival. David was known for his loose interpretation of the law in times of war and for improvising for the sake of survival. He had done so before in the case of the shewbread, and now in this situation.

What is remarkable, is that there is no blaring condemnation or judgment from God in either set of circumstances. This is just my thoughts, and you can take it for what it is worth, but I sincerely believe that God will "ALLOW" through his permissive will certain contradiction to the law in order to provide for his children for a time period. I know that I have to explain that so I will make an effort to do so. Paul describes it this way; *"All things are lawful to me but all things are not expedient: all things are lawful for me, but I will not be brought under the power of any." I Corinthians 6:12* That is the key, not being brought under the power of any. Observance of the action of David during this period indicates that he was not brought under the power and the influence of the Gods of the Philistines. His heart remained true to God and the tribe of Judah.

A brief word on the permissive will of God. First of all, it is not His Divine will. And secondly, it is only for a season. I know in my spirit that there are people out there on jobs who are paying bills and taking care of their family. Yet, you know that this is not God's will for you. The supervisor does not treat you with respect. He finds ways to mess with your raise, etc. Because of this, you say in your heart that you are going to quit and leave. Consider this in your spirit that maybe God only has you there for a season for the sake of provision. You do not have to leave right now because God will give you the grace necessary to endure it until that season is over.

David stayed in the region of the Philistines and the area of the territory called Zik lag for one year and four months. He, his family and his army had made refuge in the area and enjoyed a certain level of comfort and security there. The proximity was almost perfect. It was south of Israel and just north of Egypt. It was near to the land of the Amalekites and surrounding lands of the Geshurites, Gezrites, Moabites and Edomites. It was a staging area for the guerrilla type warfare that David and his men conducted. He made many successful raids from this area. Some of them were covert and against the land of alliance with the Philistines.

But David's season was about to change. The ***three days*** that it took him to go up with Achish to fight against Israel and return to Zik lag were about to change his season. Of course, the princes of the Philistines would not allow him to fight against Israel for fear that he would turn against them in the heat of battle. (1 Samuel 29:3-11). Nevertheless, it seems as though he was poised to fight against his own nation. From every indication of his actions then and his actions to follow, I believe he would have. Here is a man who has served Saul and all Israel valiantly, putting his life on the line time and time in battle now, only to be an outsider dwelling in the land of his enemy.

I honestly believe that David was tired. He fought for Saul and then played for him to comfort him when the evil spirit troubled him only to have a javelin cast at him. Saul chased him throughout Israel. While doing so on one occasion, he had an opportunity to kill Saul and did not. Still, Saul tried to kill him. He had forgiven every wrong and suffered long in this battle, and I believe, he was ready for it to end, even if he had to end it in battle in alliance with the enemy of his nation.

Now you and I know that it is a dangerous thing for the children of God to get tired. They do not want to hear another apology. They do not want flowers or candy. They do not want a sad song – They just want you gone. They do not want any promises of how it can be, because all they remember is how it was. When God's people get tired, all they want to do is fight. So, you had better stay clear.

We all know that it was not in the will of God for David to slay Saul, God's anointed, but as I said before, I believe he was ready. Thank God that he was withheld from the fight. Even that had to be humiliating. He had been dismissed from Saul's army and was considered a fugitive. Now, he was dismissed from the Philistine army and was given a dishonorable discharge. I am certain that this was a low point in his life, not having the opportunity to fight for what he knows is his destiny. He had to leave it in the hands of somebody else.

This was God's battle. It belonged to Him and Him alone. He had reserved the right to do the fighting for David this time and in this situation. It is never in order for brother and sisters to fight. It only makes matters worse. Our response should be to forgive the offense continually. If the oppression continues, there comes a point in time where God will step in Himself and judge the situation as well as the oppressor. When it comes to a situation like that, let God do the fighting for you.

Zik lag – Zig-Zag

"When David and his men were come to Zik lag on the **Third day**..." Zik lag, the place that had been a *fortress* or as it is so defined from the Hebrew word (*Haluza*) had now become a city laid waste. It was attacked, plundered, routed and burned. How could this place that had been the source of provision, security, comfort and joy, now be the place of sorrow, anguish, grief, desolation and loss? This place had now had its meaning reversed in three days. It had turned into what I call, Zig-Zag.

The word "Zig-Zag" refers to a winding, crisscrossing course that is followed. It is never a direct line to the destination. When I was a child, I would play a game with my sibling and neighborhood friends where we would roll a tire from an automobile on the black top roads in front of our house. We had all kinds of games we played with these tires, but one in particular would involve the zigzag motion of the tire. The idea was to make the tire zigzag as much as possible while trying to get to the end of the road without it falling over. If you could do that, then you won. I won that game a lot primarily because I learned what it took to balance my tire properly. It seemed as though I had mastered the art of zig-zag as a young child.

Since I have known the Lord and been filled with His spirit, I believe that the Lord allows us to zig-zag our way through life, at times, on our way to our destination.

For fifty years, I have worked in ministry. During that period, I have pastored, overseen churches, counseled, preached evangelistically, done missions throughout the world and worked in various community endeavors. I have observed that the people who get to their purpose in life never seem to do so in a direct line; they zig-zag. They meander, wind and crisscross on their way. I pondered the benefits of the extremes of life and one day, God spoke to me. He said to me, ***"Just like you learned balance on your tire to win the game, you must learn balance in life to win".*** It is the extremes that help you to learn the equilibriums of life. How do you know how to comfort others if you never had sorrow? How can you have empathy for someone when you never knew pain? It is our pain and our sorrows that help us to get to our purpose and in the kingdom of God, not a single painful moment of ours goes in vain. Jesus became the mediator through his temptation. Paul learned contentment through abounding and being abased. You can learn your way through your zig-zag experiences.

The Circle of Life

A few years ago, a popular movie was made called The Lion King. The soundtrack for that movie included a song that was born from inspiration. It was called The Circle of Life. In that song was depicted the search for individual purpose through despair and hope, faith and love until we find our place on the path that is unwinding that was termed the circle of life. In the previous paragraphs, I mentioned how life takes us on a winding path that zig-zags through life but that is not the ultimate intent of the Lord who guides our lives. God wants us to conquer every phase in progression and move past pediatrics to mature purpose. Needless to say, each phase of victory is seldom accomplished with one straightforward try. Usually, it takes multiple efforts.

For example, we will look at God as our instructor in the course of life. As in the case of any subject, there is preparatory study and then a test of some sort to evaluate your comprehension of the material. In the kingdom of our Lord, the primary subject is that of faith. It is the most elementary of subjects and carries through to every advanced course that will follow. Hence, if you learn this elementary course, you will not have any problems with those that remain. To accomplish this task, the Lord will use the circumstances of the circle of life to evaluate our faith.

In the exhortation of James, the brother of our Lord Jesus Christ, he encouraged all of the Christians to endure trials and temptations. *My bretheren, count it all joy when ye fall into divers temptation; Knowing this, that the trying of your faith worketh patience. But let patience have her perfect work, that you may be perfect and entire wanting nothing. James 1:2-3* The word *trying* in this passage is more accurately translated, *test* or *testing* of your faith. The psalmist made this request of the Lord, **Examine me, O Lord, and prove me: try my reins and my heart. (Psalms 26:2)** In the Amplified edition, the word try is also rendered *test*. So, it is the test of our faith that catapults us to the course of patience and when patience is mastered, we will be perfect (*mature*) and want nothing. What an amazing declaration – having no need of anything, being complete and fulfilled in this circle of life. That is our promise and our inheritance.

To obtain it, however, we must pass the test. Now, God is not an instructor like many of the instructors in the secular society. He will give you the test over and over in the circle of life until you pass it. Now, it is my prayer that you will not be as the children of Israel who went around the mountain so many times that they knew the goats by name. They were tested forty years in the wilderness with a test that could have been accomplished in a few days. The truth of the matter is this, in Gods university, you can advance at your own rate. The conditions that determine your acceleration are that of faith and obedience to the required curriculum. So, it is not necessary for us to wander aimlessly in a circle. It is time for us all to get on the straight path to recovery, restoration and success.

Seasons of Recovery

The Third Day

Another aspect of progression toward the straight path has to do with the time and the seasons of recovery. As previously stated, David spent one year and four mounts in the land of the Philistines. By the account of Achish, there was no evil found in him from the day he came to him until the day the Philistine lords dismissed him. He remained faithful to his purpose.

To understand and interpret the times and season of recovery, I will employ what I term prophetic scriptural numerology. Do not be alarmed by that principle. Prophetic scriptural numerology is the study of numbers as they are interpreted in a scriptural sense. There is a counterpart to this principle that is done in both secular and cultic activity. Nevertheless, we will not allow the practice of that which is false to deter our purpose. Prophetic scriptural numerology is based upon the principle that every number in scripture has a particular meaning and when understood in proper context, will reveal prophetic insight. By prophetic insight, I do not refer to psychic reading, but rather those prophetic promises that are both forth-told and foretold from scripture. The scripture will always be our barometer. Anything that is not in agreement with the whole word of God, will not be received. Now that we have gotten that out of the way, we will proceed.

David returned to Zik lag on the *third day*.

Three in scripture is always used to denote Divine completeness. It is the first of four perfect numbers; three, seven, ten and twelve.

- Three means Divine completeness.
- Seven, means Divine perfection.
- Ten means ordinal perfection.
- Twelve means governmental perfection.

The term 'the third day' is first mentioned in Genesis 1:13, *"And the evening and the morning were the third day"*. Therefore, we will employ the hermeneutical first mentioned principle to establish its meaning throughout the scriptures. The third day is the day in which the earth was caused to rise up out of the water. Therefore, the third day has symbolism of the completeness of resurrection. Jonah was in the belly of the fish for three days and rose from the depths of the sea to bring a complete revival to Nineveh. He was a type of Jesus Christ who rose on the third day to bring complete revival to the world. It is not to be confused with the number eight which means resurrection specifically, but three is the amount of completeness in resurrection. Jesus was raised on the third day chronologically and the eight day of Passover. So, the use of the number three and the phraseology 'the third day' denotes the completion of one event and the resurrection of another.

In Hebraic culture, numbers and alphabets have synonymous meaning. The Hebrew calendar year is 5783. The year is "3". Our Gregorian calendar 2023. The year of the Hebraic calendar and the Gregorian calendar are the same. The year is "3". The Jews believe God's calendar is revelatory to help us focus upon the prophetic significance contained in a specific season of our lives.

The Jewish calendar is set by the movements of the sun and moon, unlike our Gregorian calendar.

"And God said, Let there be lights in the firmament of the heaven to divide the day from the night; and let them be for signs, and for seasons, and for days, and years." Genesis 1:14

This scripture specifies that God placed the sun, moon and stars in the heavens for *signs* and *seasons* in our lives. In the Amplified Bible, Leviticus 23:2, calls these seven established holy times – appointed times, my appointed times are these.

"Speak to the children of Israel and say to them, 'The appointed times (established feasts) of the Lord which you shall proclaim as holy convocations – My appointed times are these: Leviticus 23:2 Amplified Bible

Throughout the Bible, God has emphasized the importance of these holy times. Jesus was crucified on Passover and fifty days later, on the day of Pentecost, the New Testament church began. In John 5:1-4, during one of these appointed holy seasons, an angel of God came down and troubled the waters causing all who stepped in first to be healed. God is a God of times, seasons and numbers.

Again, the Jews believe that these appointed times are for enhanced relationship with the Lord and a time of revelation of the purpose of God toward His people during that particular season. So, the question may be asked, what is God's revealed purpose toward His purpose in the year 5783/2023. What does God want us to know? What does God want us to see? What does God want us to do in this third year?

Gimel

The number three in Hebraic text is the alphabet *gimel* and looks like a picture of a camel. Thus, the English interpretation of *gimel* is camel. In the Hebraic culture as well as many other middle eastern cultures, the camel is thought of as a source of *supply*. In the Talmud, which is the historical writings of Israel, *gimel* is translated as a rich man running toward a poor man. It is the letter *gimel* going toward the next letter *dalet* – which translates as weakness, or poverty.

Another observation for the word camel; camel in the Hebrew is the word (*gamel*) which denotes burden bearer, to deal bountifully with a person, to repay as in judgment or reward for blessings to bring fullness of completion in Divine order.

When we look at 2023 in the Gregorian calendar and 5783 in the Hebraic calendar, each end in the number 3. If Hebraic numerical prophesy is correct and I believe it is, this is the appointed time for restoration and recovery for God's people. It is a time for the transfer of wealth, restoration, reward to the righteous and judgement to the unjust. Ref… (Proverbs 13:21-23)

We have arrived in the third season to begin again. We have come to the kingdom for such a time as this to be restored.

Please allow me to make another observation; 2015 through 2022 was a shmita period, a seven-year jubilee sabbatical period. That period ended in 2022. This year 5783/2023 is the beginning of a new cycle or a new beginning.

Behold, I will do a new thing; now it shall spring forth; shall you not know it? Isaiah 43:19

When God does a New Beginning, He brings an end to the old and starts something fresh. Let us align ourselves with the new thing that God is about to do in our lives.

In the case of David, it was the end of one season and the beginning of another. His time as a fugitive and vagabond had come to an end. It was now time to pursue another season that would propel him to the throne of the king of Israel. This was his time to be changed from a caterpillar to a butterfly. Now, you and I know that this change only occurs after the cocoon stage and David was about to experience his.

The Fire at Zik lag

Zik lag was burned with fire. As David and his men neared the city, it is likely that they saw plumes of smoke billowing into the air. Well before they arrived, the anxiety increased as he and the men wondered what calamity had overtaken their village and their property and most importantly their wives and children. The closer they got, the more agony they felt. Then finally in plain view, they could see. Their village was burned with fire. No one was present. Even though their wives and children were not present, every one of them were in dismay. Were they alive still? Had they taken them somewhere near to slaughter them? Were they maimed or tortured and raped? What had befallen them in the three days they were gone?

What a melancholy state of despair the men found themselves in? Fire has a way of finality to it. It reduces everything that it touches to ashes that have no redeeming value. All kind of questions filled their minds. Was God still for them? How could they ever recover? What good could come out of this fire?

To answer this question, let me share with you an experience that happened to me while I was traveling to London. I had some down time between my next conference in Ghana, Africa so, I decided to spend some time in London. I did a little shopping for souvenirs and went sightseeing on the double deck bus tour. While on the tour, the guide began to relate a story concerning the great fire of London. There had been a massive outbreak of bubonic plague in the years 1665 – 1666. In the Kingdom of England, it is estimated that 100,000 people died, 20 per cent of London's population. Records state that the death rate spiraled from 1000 a week to two thousand and by September 1665, to seven thousand people per week. Then on September 2 and 3, the Great fire of London destroyed much of the center of London and people began to notice that the plague had tapered off. After the fire, people noticed that the fire had gotten so hot that it burned the rats in the sewer and killed even the fleas on the rats.

The disease itself is an infection by the bacterium Yersinia pestis, transmitted through a flea vector.

God spoke to me through this story. Sometimes, God allows the fire into our lives as a purification to burn up the rats and even the fleas because where we are going in the next phase of our lives, we have no room for rats or fleas. We cannot take rats or fleas with us into our new season.

Yes, the fire burned Zik lag, but it started a new beginning in the life of David. It will also do the same for everyone who will totally trust in God to direct their lives toward the new beginning He has for us. All of our new beginnings may not be the way we think they should be. For some of us, the challenges may be great. I said at the beginning that this season has been a season of loss where many have faced foreclosures, higher gas prices and food prices. Energy prices have soared, jobs have been lost and changes have to be made as we approach everyday living. Hopefully though, some of our new beginnings will cause us to trust God and will thrust us into a greater dependence upon Him where we may excel to a higher level of success.

The Season of Change

To every thing there is a season, and a time to every purpose under the heaven: (Eccl. 3:1)

Sometimes, when things are the worse, God is ending one season and beginning another. These seasons and times are referred to respectively as kronos and kairos. Kronos refers to general or chronological time periods, and Kairos refers to the specific time periods in which extraordinary things are at work moving us toward our specific purpose.

God began speaking to me through numerical prophesy in 2008 concerning the body of Christ and various seasons of change. I acknowledge that much of the prophesy was very personal and dealing with my particular walk with God. I also concede that some details were applicable to the Body of Christ in general. He began dealing with me in seasons of seven-year spans from 2008 – 2015, 2015 – 2022. God spoke different promises of every season. Each year He would give me a theme to follow and an assignment to go along with the theme. In the first year of the season, the Lord said to me that this season would be a categorized as a time of resurrection for the covenant people of God. It definitely was so in my life. The numerical prophesy of 2008 can be broken down into the understanding of the number two. Two is a number for covenant. It takes two to make a covenant. therefore, two stands for the covenant people of God. Eight is the number of resurrections. When put together, the number denotes a time of resurrection for the covenant people of God.

This went on for fourteen years, (two seven-year periods). During those years, I fought to maintain the purpose of God in my life and ministry. I felt the perils of Paul: Perils in my journeys; perils among robbers; perils among people I had known most of my adult life; perils in the city; perils in the country and perils among false brethren. I must admit that there were times that I did not hear God clearly and when I did, I did not always comprehend the complete message of His will. I felt like Sophia in 'Color Purple' "All My Life I Had to Fight".

However, I kept fighting and kept moving forward in faith.

Now, 2023, is the third season that is beginning a new cycle. At the beginning of this third cycle of sabbatical years, 2023, I clearly hear the theme for this year. This is the word I have been waiting for the last fourteen years. I call it the season of "RE"! RE, for me, it is RESTORATION! It is reward. It is recovery. It is redemption. You can add the suffix to whatever your faith allows.

Obstacles to Recovery

As David faced obstacles in his new season of recovery, so will we, and if we are to win, we must overcome the most common obstacles:

Judgment – Captivity – Grief – Despair – Betrayal – Negative Public Opinion – Discouragement

Let us see how he dealt with them. The confusion and consternation that David and his men found themselves in when they returned was almost unbearable. Their houses were in ashes and their wives and children were gone into captivity. They had marched for three days from the camp of the Philistines to Zik lag, with the expectation of finding rest in their houses and joy in their families. A dismal scene was presented to them which made all of them weep to the point that they had no more power to weep. The passage said that David and all of the men with him wept. These were not mere sobbing, but they were whaling's of anguish and screams of pain. Not only did David have to deal with his own grief, but he had to deal with the grief of the men as well. They acerbated his grief by blaming him to the point they spoke of stoning him. These men did not grieve in silence. He was the brunt of their conversation and the shout of their voices. Their grief turned to anger with contemplation of violence. Their thoughts were not on recovery, but upon blaming David for their misfortune and loss. They seem to care more about finding a scapegoat than solving the problem at hand.

David had to somehow manage to get a moment of solitude long enough to compose himself and look for a solution. He knew perfectly well that fire and captivity were instruments of judgment and now he had to deal with the grief of personal and corporate loss as well as the despair of the future. There is no account that those whom he had given meaning to life were there to assist him. He had no support from the men. Isn't it strange that when you are giving people what they want, they love you, but the moment trouble comes, those same people abandon and betray you?

Methodology of Recovery

Self-Courage

The first step to recovery is courage, but how do you encourage yourself when everything has the appearance that it is all over; that there is no hope of the future; that family is gone; money is gone, and all of your life savings is gone. Courage comes from God so; you must look to God. David knew where courage and help came from so, he looked to the hills of the Lord. Perhaps, he spoke to his soul and asked his soul why he was disquieted within himself. Didn't his soul remember that God had brought him this far? Didn't he remember that his help and hope was in God? Could David hear the inner man within him saying, "God is a very present help in the time of trouble?" I believe that he said many things to himself about his experiences with God that gave him motivation to go forward. This was his style. When he faced Goliath, he recounted the experience of the lion and the bear and projected his faith into the future. This in essence is the secret to self-courage. Looking to the past with reflections only brings nostalgia whether good or bad, but looking to the past motivation to look beyond the present to the future will always empower. We must always focus upon the next move of God in our lives. That is the catalyst for courage.

Overcoming Grief

Before you can hear clear direction from God, you must deal with grief. This brief excerpt of a guide that I use in counseling is for an extended period of grief from six weeks to approximately four years. It is not the full guide, but for any reader going through grief, I have included it. These are not all of the steps, but it is a good start. Be comforted.

I. **Cry**: Crying releases oxytocin and endogenous opioids also known as endorphins. These are feel good chemicals to help ease both physical and emotional pain. We relieve our body of toxins and hormones like cortisol that contribute to elevated stress levels. This will help us to sleep better, which helps to strengthen our immune system, lower our stress levels and lower your blood pressure. Crying also produces a calming effect afterwards and helps to regulate our emotions.

II. **Do not blame yourself**: The Devil is an accuser of the people of God and his first response in a situation of grief is to inflict pain by bringing thought to your mind that in some way you are the cause.

During this period, you may also blame others and even blame God. This is never productive and causes additional pain.

III. **Encourage yourself.**

A. Literally talk to yourself about you.

B. Find your purpose in life.

C. Do something for yourself that means a lot to you that you failed to do in the past.

IV. **Pray**

A. Pray with a fervent and sincere intent and ask God to take the pain away.

V. **Praise**

A. Develop a daily routine (preferably in the morning) of giving God thanks for the good.

VI. **Think about the good times.**

A. Jot down some things on a piece of paper, in the form of a letter or journal.

B. Make banners or picture album to reflect on

VII. **Memorialize your loved ones.**

A. There are numerous ways to do this. Find one that appeals to you.

VIII. Get moving:

A. Do some form of physical activity.

B. Get involved in some form of social activity.

C. Get a part time job or volunteer for an event that is important to you.

IX.   Discover alternate sources of joy.

A. Pour your love into other family members.

B. Keep good people around you.

X.   Live a life of purpose.

A. Travel.

B. Enjoy family gatherings, reunions, family picnics!

Intercession

  Unfortunately, David and his men did not have the time to grieve properly in a state of battle, so they had to urgently get on with the task of recovering. What did he do? I suggest you do the same.

  Talk to the priest. I say that in a metaphorical sense. I do not practice the catholic faith and that is not a railing accusation of condemnation against that faith. I speak of priest as an intercessor, a prayer warrior and a confidant. That does not necessarily have to be the one that is dressed in holy garb who talks to you from behind a confession booth. I say that to indicate that every leader, every person needs someone who can pray to God with them and talk to you when you are in trouble. Every Bishop and Pastor needs someone that will hear them and not condemn them. Sometimes they do not have to say a word. They can just be there to listen to the contents of their heart. They can be an intercessor for them between the situation and God.

Abiathar was David's priest. Just to call his name had to be courage to David, because his name meant the father of abundance, or my father excels. God was the father of David, and he was the father of abundance not loss, the father who excels not fails. Praise God for true priest! Always have people around you that will engage with you in corporate prayer and will hold your hands up in encouragement.

I remember a certain sister in the first church that I founded. Her name was Sister Scott. She was not an officer or minister. As a matter of fact, she was an usher. She was seemingly insignificant to many of the members. After every service, she would make it her business to wait around for me before I left the building just to say, "Be encouraged!" That meant the world to me. After a while, I found myself making my way to her just to hear those two words. Everybody needs a Sister Scott in their lives. Make sure you have one.

The Ephod

"Bring me the Ephod". The Ephod was a sacred linen garment worn by the high priest of Israel. It was in two parts – one covering the back, one covering the front of the body to the hips—and was fasten at the shoulders by two clasps on onyx on which were engraved the twelve tribal names, six on each. The vestment was held in at the waist by a twined linen girdle of gold, blue, purple and scarlet; on the ephod was the breastplate with the Urim and Thummin, hung by golden chains and rings. The priest was adorned in this fashion to symbolize the presence of God with his people.

Prophetic Prayer

No theologian has been able to determine just how the Ephod with the Urim and Thummin were used to see prophetically into the mind of God and into their future state. I will not venture to teach the theologians but will advance a premise. Isaiah speaks of ... "the garment of praise for the spirit of heaviness". (Isaiah 61:3). I will not venture to say that this was the ephod garment, but I will say that praise was the instrument for insight and the preface to prophetic understanding.

Praise sets the tone to invoke the presence of God. Praise destroys the demonic atmosphere of heaviness, grief, despair and suicide and ushers in the atmosphere of faith and victory. It then enables us to pray the will of God for our lives through prophetic revelation. David understood this. He had written a psalm about it:

"But thou art holy, O thou that inhabitest the praise of Israel" Psalms 22:3

Prior to arriving at that conclusion, David was complaining to God about being forsaken, being distant from him and not helping him while he was as his psalm said, "roaring". The Hebrew word here is *seaga* meaning a rumbling or moan as the roar of a lion or a cry of distress. As long as David was complaining, feeling forsaken, feeling helpless and roaring at God, his prayers went unanswered. However, in the middle of all of David's pity party, he remembered that God was holy (*kadosh*) i.e., different, set apart, and did not respond to the moaning, complaining, crying and roaring of mankind in prayers. He only responds to the praises of Israel.

The Praises of Israel

- There are seven distinct praises that the Israelites practiced, and the psalmist said that God inhabits those praises. The first one is <u>**HALAL**</u> – 'haw-lal' - This word appears over 110 times in the OT. To be clear, to shine; hence, to make a show, to boast; and thus, to be (clamorously) foolish; to rave; causatively, to celebrate; also, to stultify:

  Scriptures: 1 Chron. 16:4, 23:5,30, 25:3, 29:13, Neh. 12:24

- <u>*YADAH*</u> – 'yaw-daw' - to worship with the extended hand. The giving of oneself in worship and adoration. To lift your hands unto the Lord. It carries the meaning of absolute surrender as a young child does to a parent - "pick me up, I'm all yours".

Scriptures: Gen. 29:35, 2 Chron. 7:6, 20:21, Psalms 9:1, 28:7, Psalms 33:2, 42:5,11, 49:18, Isaiah 12:1

- <u>*TOWDAH*</u> – 'to-daw' - To give worship by the extension of the hand in adoration or agreeing with what has been done or will be. This word is commonly found in connection with sacrifice-applying the giving of thanks or praise as a sacrifice before reception or manifestation. Thanking God for something that I do not have in the natural. Agreeing with His Word - faith in His Word. This form of praise goes into operation just because His Word is true. "Father, I thank YOU that YOUR WORD is TRUE. But there is great faith in *TOWDAH* as praise." The lifting of the hand symbolizes agreement. The right hand symbolizes my covenant with my Father.

- <u>*SHABACH*</u> – 'shaw-bakh' - to address in a loud tone, a loud adoration, a shout! Proclaim with a loud voice, unashamed, the GLORY, TRIUMPH, POWER, MERCY, LOVE OF GOD. This word implies that testimony is praise. The phrase "shout unto the Lord" can be understood as the action of *SHABACH*. It is not just being loud. You should have the attitude of putting your whole being into it, an attitude of being totally uninhibited.

  Scriptures: Psalm 117:1, 63:3-4

- <u>BARAK</u> – 'baw-rak' - To kneel or to bow. To give reverence to God as an act of adoration. It implies to continual conscious giving place to God. Blessing the Lord, extolling virtue. There is a sense of kneeling and blessing God as an act of adoration in the word BARAK. Physical application - To bow, kneel or to do this with the intent in my heart that He is my KING and I yield to HIM. I am acknowledging Him as KING and GOD.

  Scripture: Psalm 103

- <u>ZAMAR</u> – 'zaw-mar' - To sing with instruments. To make music accompanied by the voice. One of the musical verbs for praise in the book of psalms. It carries the idea of making music in praise to God as in Psalm 92:1. The word *ZAMAR* also means to touch the strings and refers to praise that involves instrumental worship as in Psalm 150. The one word is usually translated "sing praises".

- <u>TEHILLAH</u> – is derived from the word halal and means "The singing of halals, to sing or to laud; perceived to involve music, especially singing; hymns of the Spirit or praise."

    Psalms 22:3, "But thou art holy, O Thou who inhabitest (are enthroned upon) the praises (*tehillah*) of Israel.,"

    Isaiah 61:3 - To grant to those who mourn in Zion, to give them beauty for ashes, the oil of joy for mourning, the garment of praise (tehillah) for the spirit of heaviness; that they may be called the trees of righteousness, the planting of the Lord that He might be glorified.

The Tehillah praise is a warfare praise that should be employed especially when encountering multiple enemies. This type of praise saturates the atmosphere with an angelic presence to defeat the spirit of despair and brings inspiration, and encouragement toward purpose.

Other Scriptural References: Exodus 15:11; Deuteronomy 10:21; Nehemiah 9:5; Psalms 9;14, 22:25; Jeremiah 48;2

Why we praise:

- We praise to bless God.
- We praise to receive blessings from God.
- We praise to transform our character.
- We praise to eliminate anxiety and depression.
- We praise to gain peace of mind.
- We praise to create a spiritual atmosphere.
- We praise to invoke the habitation of God.

We praise to destroy strongholds.

God's Answer

David prayed a prophetic prayer. Shall I pursue after this troop? Shall I overtake them? That was David's prayer, but what was spoken next was the Lord's answer. Whatever was said, next was from the Lord himself, therefore it has application not only to this specific situation, but to all who will receive its command by faith.

God's answer is:

- **Pursue.**
- **You shall overtake them.**
- **You will not fail.**
- **You will recover all.**

These are eternal words, spoken by the Lord of Glory and they are directive words to be received in faith. These directives seem simple enough but let us look closer.

Pursue means to follow, chase or hunt but implies much more. In order to pursue especially in this weakened state, it implied courage, determination, strength of mind, resolve and fortitude enough to accomplish the purpose at hand. It meant that he and his men had to wipe their tears, set aside their anger and grief and get ready for a fight. These people were three days ahead of them and they were tired physically, emotionally and spiritually. Yet they had to pursue. It is an act of faith and obedience.

You will overtake them; no matter how far your enemies are ahead of you; no matter how they have envied you and fought against you. You will surpass them and go beyond them and what they have accomplished. You will take them by surprise and sweep over them like a flood of waters and engulf them.

You will not fail; You will be successful and make the grade. You will not break down or fall short in anything, but you will thrive. You will have victory and not defeat.

You will recover all! You will recapture and repossess all that was taken from you. When the end of the story is written, everything you had will be in your hands again. In addition, you will have more because of the experience that you have gained with God. Now, you have all of the elements for recovery inside of you. You have the wisdom for the prevention of loss and the methodology for success. You shall have it all!

Find your Egyptian!

There is one thing that I noticed about God. He gives directives and he gives insight and encouragement to find your way back to recovery, but He does not give you everything you need before you move into action. He always reserves a ram in the bush or in this case, an Egyptian in the field. This tenet is what I call "Finding your Egyptian". It is finding that person to give you directions to your place of recovery. I spoke at length about individual efforts that would bring you to corporate celebration in a previous chapter. That is good in the shepherd's field with the sheep. It is good in the house with the coin. For the greater Kingdom things, you will need help to get to where God is moving you in this next phase of your life. Many feel that they can do it on their own, but everyone needs a mentor, a person whom they can be accountable to in order to guide them into areas of which they are not aware.

This is an order of God that I call the Gabriel order. I believe Gabriel to be the arc angel of the message order. When the children of God need a message from the throne, it either comes directly from the Lord himself in exceptional cases or it comes from the order of Gabriel. To find your way back to recovery will take Divine guidance. Recovery is not easy. With the barrage of emotions that a person has to deal with; with the outward opposition and principalities they have to fight; if they do not get Divine wisdom, they will not get back.

Mentoring

Some may not believe it, but we have angels assigned to us individually to assist us in whatever capacity we have need of. What we must do is solicit and command their help in prayer and direction. To unbelievers of the Gabriel order, you are depriving yourself of vital information necessary to the restoration of your full purpose. God has a person, a mentor, to help you that has been commissioned through this order. How dare you feel like you know it all or can do it all and want to spend it all. Hear, my words spoken as clear as can be. Find your Egyptian.

How do you know where to look for your Egyptian? First, you must have a clear pursuit and a proper objective. The clarity of pursuit will come from your passion and the gifting that is already in you. By that, I mean you have in you a desire to be this special person, do this certain thing and have this certain way of life and living. It is your passion, your dream and your purpose in life. Guess what! There is somebody that has already done what you want to do. Why reinvent the wheel when it has already been invented? Just find your Egyptian (your mentor) to propel you to your destiny.

Coincidence or Purpose

Did they just happen to come upon the Egyptian? I tell you, no, it was not a coincidence. They were doing what God had told them to do, *pursue*. It was in their pursuit that they found the Egyptian. They would have never found him had they not begun the pursuit, or had they stopped the pursuit before they found further direction. He got sick three days earlier. Why do you think he got sick? His masters decided to leave him there. Why was it in their hearts to leave him there to die? There are no coincidences with God, only purposes. Once He tells you to do something, He will direct you on to the end of it.

Gifts

Just a small note here on how they got the information from the Egyptian; they gave him gifts. They gave him bread and they made him drink water. They gave him a piece of cake of figs, and two clusters of raisins. They gave him the promise of life. They wanted information and he had the information they needed. They were willing to share their gift in order to secure the information that would ensure their recovery. It was a small price to pay for the recovery of all of their stuff. That is not to say that it was not sacrificial. It was because they had just lost so much. But as the prophet said to David, I will not receive of the Lord that which cost me nothing. If your mentor is willing to share his gift, then you should share yours. "If you give me gifts, I will bring you down to this company".

The Six Hundred

In the case of David and his six hundred men, they pursued hard after the enemy from Zik lag to Besor. Two hundred of the men were so faint that they could not cross over the brook Besor and David did not throw them away or kick them out of his army. He could have. Some of them were probably among the number that wanted to stone him.

He did not just leave them, but he delegated them to new assignments. These were warriors but they were at this point so faint that they could not go any further to fight. David instituted a new law that later became known as David's law that required them to watch over the stuff.

The brook Besor means "cool refreshing." Those who could not go any further found what they needed, cool refreshing water. They found rest both for their bodies and their minds.

Six hundred men began the journey to recover all. Six is the number of men. At this point in my ministry, I recognize that numbers in scripture are not just fortuitous. They always have a deeper purpose for being sited. I believe God wanted to show David that this recovery was God ordained, and though he and his men were willing to be collaborative in the effort of restoration and recovery, this was an intentionality in His divine will, and he was going to show his hand for victory on their behalf. God would not have them to be delivered by the strength of men in this case. Even if He had to reduce the army by a *third*. Somebody caught that. Remember what I said about God's use of the number three.

Two hundred were left. This puts you in mind of God reducing the army of Gideon so He and only He would get the glory. That, however, is another story. Incidentally, the numerical understanding of two hundred is symbolic of covenant. So, even though they were on different assignments, they were still in covenant.

The Four Hundred

Nevertheless, those four hundred continued with David to the battle. This was a God mandate. Four hundred is the number of prosperities of the earth. It also has another meaning to suggest a period of testing before inheritance. The children of Israel were four hundred years in Egypt. Jesus was 40 days in the wilderness, etc. Throughout this whole ordeal, God was intent on showing his hand to prosper David and his group even if their faith had to be tested. The four hundred found what they needed, the Egyptian. This may sound harsh, but it is true. There are some people in the kingdom who will not receive the mentoring of the Egyptian. They do not aspire to be mentored to any depth other than that of Besor, cool refreshing. Thus, they will not receive a mentor. If God dropped down one from the sky, they would not receive them. Some people are meant to guard the stuff, and I do not say that disrespectful. That is their function in the kingdom, and they will be rewarded for their service. I do not know whether you are a 200 or a 400 but I say to you, "Do what you are purposed to do".

The Battle for Recovery

All is set. The Egyptian has brought them down to the camp of the Amalekites. The Amalekites are totally unaware of impending defeat. Instead, they are spread abroad, not in a battle formation or a battle frame of mind. They are eating, drinking, and dancing. They were most likely drunk. Surely though, they were unprepared. Here is another principle that might be observed to keep you from losing your stuff. *Revelry and indulgence are a practice that leads to poverty.* Ref...Proverbs 11:24 You cannot eat the seed and expect a harvest! Those are just wisdom nuggets for your consideration.

The Strategy for Battle

The strategy for the battle is set by God. This was a new strategy. It was out of the ordinary for a battle to be engaged in the twilight of the evening prior to this time. Soldiers depended heavily upon the light of the sun and would wait until the dawn to begin the battle. This battle has a sense of urgency; therefore, the time of recovery is accelerated by beginning the fight in the eve of night and fighting until the evening of the next day. If you want to recover all and experience total restoration, understand the sense of urgency and denounce procrastination.

Look for just a minute at the symbolism here. They fought through the twilight and through the midnight. Twilight is the boundary between day and night. It is indicative of a barrier. This barrier was not previously crossed in battle because there was no night vision goggles to see by. Evidently, God was their light!

Midnight is when one day ends and another begins. In scripture, midnight occurs fourteen times and is always associated with some demonstration of the power of God either in judgment, salvation, or deliverance. At midnight, God judged the Egyptian and delivered the Israelites. (Exodus 11:4; 12:29) At midnight, Paul and Silas sang praises in a Philippian jail and God sent an earthquake to deliver them which resulted in their freedom and the salvation of the Philippian jailer and his family. (Acts 16:25-28). The symbolism of midnight is the end of one day or period or season and the new beginning of another day or period. For those experiencing twilight or midnight in their lives, please know that a new day is coming. Keep on fighting!

They fought for the span of a day, but they fought through the duration of the night to gain the victory in the twilight of the next day. That means that they fought through the midnight hour and even into the darkest hour before daybreak. Urgency for recovery requires this type of strategy. Nevertheless, the reward is always worth the fight.

Total Recovery For All

David recovered all! He rescued his family, his wives, sons and daughters. ***There was nothing that was lacking to him or to the men that were allied to him.*** He took back everything that was taken; all the flocks and the herds of cattle. In addition, David took additional spoil of the Amalekites. God spoke a few things into my spirit:

- God will give you more than you lost – double for your shame.

- "Everyone that is connected to the leader's spirit, will prosper when the leader prospers."

Everyone was rewarded. The four hundred that fought and the two hundred that stayed with the stuff.

David's New Law

A new law of preservation was instituted to preserve the property as a result of the two hundred. There would always be someone watching over the property, and they would receive the same reward as those who fought. These were support soldiers and their duty was equated as the same as those who fought on the front lines. This practice, although implemented by David, is taught and employed to this day in military warfare. It is called combat support troops. They provide fire support and operational assistance to combat elements. They provide specialized support functions to combat units in such areas as engineering, intelligence, security and communications.

David began the battle in prayer and praise and was careful to end the victory the same way. His praise was for God as *a provider, a preserver* and *a deliverer*:

"The Lord has given! The Lord has preserved! The Lord has delivered!"

David understood another principle that needs to be renumerated, when God blesses you with recovery and restoration, be sure to put a praise on it. I say, seal it with a praise so the devil cannot steal it. Always put a praise on it.

Overflow

David also followed another principle that ensures continual blessing, recovery and restoration. He gave to Judah, his friends, to those Athach, Bethel, Ramoth, Jattir, Aroer, Siphmoth, Eshtemoa, Rachal, the cities of the Jerahmelites, the cities of the Kenites, at Chorashan, in Hebron and to every place where he and his men were accustomed to go.

Why would David give away so much? Perhaps, it was assurance, or ingratiating to gain favor. Maybe it was just a gift. Whatever the reason, there is something to be learned. If you give, you shall surely receive, pressed down, running over and men will give into your bosom. God will continually open windows and doors of opportunity for you to be blessed. Your children and grandchildren will be blessed.

And if by chance you lose in the future, **YOU WILL RECOVER ALL!**

Made in the USA
Monee, IL
29 August 2023